MIRACLE VALLEY 3

THE ONGOING STORY OF HOLLYBUSH FARM & FELLOWSHIP

Jim Wilkinson

& Mark McKnight

McKnight
& Bishop
Ltd
Inspire

ABOUT THE PUBLISHER

McKnight & Bishop are always on the lookout for great new authors and ideas for exciting new books. If you write or if you have an idea for a book, email us:

info@mcknightbishop.com

Some things we love are: undiscovered authors, open-source software, crowd-funding, Amazon/Kindle, social networking, faith, laughter and new ideas.

Visit us at: **www.mcknightbishop.com**

Scripture quotations marked (NIV) are taken from the Holy Bible, New International Version®, NIV®. Copyright © 1973, 1978, 1984, 2011 by Biblica, Inc.™ Used by permission of Zondervan. All rights reserved worldwide. www.zondervan.com The "NIV" and "New International Version" are trademarks registered in the United States Patent and Trademark Office by Biblica, Inc.™

ISBN 978-1-905691-34-0

A CIP catalogue record for this book is available from the British Library

First published in 2015 by McKnight & Bishop Inspire, an imprint of:

McKnight & Bishop Ltd.
28 Grifffiths Court, Bowburn, Co. Durham, DH6 5FD
http://www.mcknightbishop.com
info@mcknightbishop .com

This book has been typeset in Garamond-Normal

Printed and bound in Great Britain by The Printing House, London

CONTENTS

I dedicate this book in thanksgiving to the love, care, comfort and prayer of my dear wife, Cynthia. She has been my companion on this journey for 57 years. Up until these last few months, we have almost always travelled as a team.

Thank you, Lord and thank you Cynthia.

I also acknowledge a debt of thanks to everyone who has been and those who are still dedicated to the original and unchanged prophetic word: "I will bring people from the north, south, east and west to minister to you and be ministered to."

Our task has been and now is to provide the means for it to happen.

INTRODUCTION

The stories of Hollybush past, present and future aren't told on any web-page. When you fire up Google and search for 'Hollybush,' it will point you to a garden centre in Stafford, a pub in Northumberland and a B&B in Ayrshire. And if you search for long enough, you'll find the tiny community of Hollybush, Kentucky, USA.

Hollybush Christian Fellowship is in there somewhere – quiet, unassuming, not trumpeting its achievements or aggressively pursuing followers on social media. In fact, it doesn't even have a Facebook page or a Twitter account. There's a website that to my knowledge hasn't had a revamp for about ten years. Watching Jim in the office, it seems like he has only grudgingly come to accept that he will have to use email to get by.

During a Friday night meeting, look up on the stage and you won't see the beautiful young worship leaders that grace the stages of the mega churches – these are men and women no longer in their twenties. Some are no longer in their sixties. Ernest used to play his trumpet standing but the years have got the better of him and now he plays seated. The Hammond organ whose sound fills the sanctuary was built in the 1970s.

And Jim... Well, Jim is racking up the years too. Not that he seems to be showing any signs of slowing down, you understand.

In spite of all of this, Hollybush has stayed the distance. It's been a part of the landscape of this part of Yorkshire since before I was born. More importantly, it's been part of what God's Holy Spirit has been doing in this country and the world. The worship leaders might not have the latest haircut, but the worship is Spirit-filled nonetheless.

The story of Hollybush Farm's beginning was told in two editions of the book, *Miracle Valley*. That book began with the stories of some of the 'hopeless cases' that Jim and Cynthia Wilkinson have come across over the years and how God miraculously intervened. Nowadays, Jim doesn't seem to tell so many of those stories. Not because they aren't happening, you understand. I think it's because they've become so used to God's healing power at Hollybush that what you and I would call the miraculous, the folks at Hollybush just see as 'every day.'

Bernard is a great example – I met Bernard and his wife Annette on one of my first visits to Hollybush; a wonderful, warm couple who were more than happy to sit down and tell me their story over a cup of tea and some cake. Except as time went by, it became apparent that Bernard was quite seriously ill. Soon it was only Annette that I'd see around the farm and she'd tell me how Bernard was doing. And it wasn't good. The doctors had more or less decided that they were going to have to amputate his foot.

I had spent all Friday afternoon on the farm – an hour and a half putting the world to rights with Joanna and then two hours in Jim's sitting room looking out over the land and watching a storm coming in from Thirsk. There was no mention of Bernard. Just when I was leaving, I bumped into Annette and I glumly asked her how Bernard was doing.

"He's totally healed. It was a few weeks ago on the last night of camp. Isn't it wonderful? Hallelujah!"

When I found him a few moments later, Bernard was up a ladder stripping wallpaper in Irene's cottage (one of the farm buildings).

Should I have expected a healing to be the end of this story? Jim would say, "Of course! Hallelujah!" In fact, Jim could fill this book ten times over telling stories of God's healing and the wonder-working power of the Holy Spirit that he's seen at Hollybush and elsewhere. The people who were around in the very early days tell me that Miracle Valley the book doesn't really do justice to what was happening in those days: the manifestation of the Holy Spirit in the lives of everyday Yorkshire folks was beyond what anybody had ever experienced before. But Miracle Valley, as an unofficial name for this place is a fairly accurate description.

Why is it called Hollybush Farm? "Well the big house is called Hollin Tree House. Because there were some Holly bushes around. I don't know whether they planted them or not because it was before my time. They built the big house in 1928. The trees round and about weren't as high when we came here – they were about the same height as the ground floor ceilings. So in 47 years they've grown up a right bit," reminisces Jim. With all that the Holy Spirit has done on and through this farm, it ought to be called Miracle Valley Holy Ghost Revival Jubilee Anointed Christ The King Hallelujah Praise Miraculous Healing Centre!

It's telling of Jim's character that the place has never had a name change. Jim is one of the most genuine, humble, gentle, godly, Spirit-filled men you will ever meet.

There are still copies of *Miracle Valley* to be had if you know where to look. If you want to know that story, you should buy that book. It will tell you all about how Jim and Cynthia Wilkinson came to know the Lord, how they received the Holy Spirit and how they came to Hollybush Farm in 1968.

This book will tell you some of that too, but what's more exciting is the present and the future. Jim and everyone at Hollybush believe that the prophecy has only been fulfilled in part. We still wait with bated breath to see what God is going to do next. Jim, Cynthia, Joanna and the rest of Hollybush Fellowship keep asking the question: We know what God has already done, but what is he about to do? What is he going to do on this farm and with these people in the next decades?

The last we heard from Hollybush in *Miracle Valley*, foot and mouth was devastating the farming community. Since then, they've had to cope with the continued export ban (until 2006) on

British beef because of BSE. Added to that, they've had swine flu, bird flu and tuberculosis in cattle. Fierce international competition for all crops has led to very low prices. Legislation and red tape have slowed economic recovery although it has created much better welfare conditions for a lot of animals.

In the last ten years, Jim's beloved Methodist Church has lost nearly a third of its membership nationally. Snape Methodist Chapel (where Jim grew up) claimed only 42 members in 2013. There were more members in the youth group when Jim was a lad! A rampantly secular media and a liberal facing government chip away at what might be described as 'traditional Christian values.' There has been a significant cultural shift in the religious character of our nation: Christianity is in decline across most denominations while Islam and other faiths are recording increases with significant immigration particularly from Islamic countries.

And yet at Hollybush Farm, Jim and others continue to tell the stories of God's faithfulness. In spite of the decline throughout most of the rest of Christendom, Hollybush is still here and still filled with people looking for what God is doing next.

Recently I spoke to a vicar who said, "Hollybush isn't really my thing, but it does seem to have lasted where others haven't. Lots of times these big pentecostal things are a bit of a flash in the pan – they kick off, have meetings every night of the week for six months and build themselves a nice big church building. You go back five years later and there's thirty people rattling round a six hundred seat sanctuary remembering what it was like in the glory days. But there's something different about Hollybush…"

What's the difference? Well, if I knew the answer to that, I'd write a book about it. Oh wait…

Part of the reason that Hollybush has stayed the distance is that they've held on to prophecies like Roger Teale's from 1978:

1978 Prophecy

"It shall be," saith the Lord, "concerning this ministry and this place; have I not written it and did I not speak to my servant – did I not stop him in the way and speak unto him concerning the thing which I would cause him to do with his hands; and did he not meditate on it and did he not consider and refer it to his loved one; did they not refer it to one another and said, 'Surely this would be the way the Lord would work?'"

"This man has been faithful and I have blessed him and I have vowed that my presence shall be here in this place, and even the new place that I shall build. Surely they shall come from the East and the West, and from the North and the South, and surely thou shall know even that my Spirit is upon this place. It shall be known as a place of deliverance. Therefore, those that shall speak against this ministry, their mouths shall be stopped, and those that rise up, thou shalt condemn, for no weapon that is formed against thee shall prosper; therefore doubt thou not my servant – doubt me not my children. For thou hast seen my power in this place, wherefore dost thou doubt, wherefore dost thou say, 'Is it the Lord?' Or why be this seal upon this place and this ministry and surely I shall work a wonder in this place. They shall surely come, the whole earth shall know of this place. It shall be a place of fruitfulness. The needy shall be blessed and those that have needs, they shall be met," saith the Lord.

"Thou shalt also minister to the hungry, and thou shalt minister to these even in the practical. It shall be, for I shall make this place a pillar – this place shall reach up to the heavens and my word shall be declared from this place, for I shall send in those that I will anoint and I will speak, and yea my son, I have spoken unto thee this beforetime – therefore remember this, that thou shalt have a witness within thyself whom thou should have to speak and who should not, and if they speak that which is contrary to the witness I have put within thy heart and within thy very breast, stand upon thy feet and ask them to sit down and be quiet. For surely I will have my word declared in righteousness in this place, that I have ordained, for surely it shall bring healing to this nation and the nations of the world."

"Concerning the finances of this venture, surely it shall come and it shall come in large and small amounts, but yea, thou shalt have no lack, and thou must not skimp in anything thou shalt do but thou shalt have the best for me," saith the Lord. "I require the best – the carpet, the best chairs, and curtains and all that thou shalt see and behold with thine eyes, and behold thou shalt not tempt the Lord thy God by saying, 'we cannot afford it.' I will provide for my house and there shall be meat and drink and there shall be honour. People shall walk in and open their eyes and say, 'Such beauty, such glory, such things; surely the Lord hath done great things,' for will I have my testimony to be abased? Would I have that which is impoverished; would I have that which is faulty? No, it would not bring glory unto my name, I require the best. Thou must take up the choicest that it shall be before me and it shall bring honour unto my name."

In Modern Language

The Lord says, "This is how it's going to be for this ministry and this place; I've written it down and I've spoken to my servant. I've told him about the work of his hands which he's carefully thought through and talked to his wife. They've decided, this sounds like the God that we know and serve."

"This man has been faithful and I have blessed him. So I've promised that my presence will be here both now and in the future as the ministry grows. People are going to come from all over – from every direction and you'll know that my Spirit rests on this place. It will be known as a place of deliverance; freedom from everything that holds people back."

"You should know that everyone who speaks out against this

ministry will be silenced. Everyone who tries to bring it down shall be stopped. There's no weapon that can damage or destroy what I'm building here."

"You've already seen my power at work. There's no reason to doubt what I'm doing. Why are you asking, 'Is this the Lord?' Of course it is - you've seen it before and you'll see it again! And what you've yet to see will be more wonderful still."

"I'm going to demonstrate the fruits of my Spirit here: love, joy, peace, patience, kindness and lots more beside. Why? Because it's a needy and hurting world. I'm not just going to use this place to meet needs. Oh, of course we'll feed the hungry and clothe the naked but we'll do so much more than that - we're going to bless them too. Tell them the good news and that they can have some of this joy too."

"This place will be a 'thin place,' known worldwide as one of those places where the distance between heaven and earth seems a whole lot closer. I'm going to send men and women of God that I have anointed to speak to you. Occasionally someone will come along that says something at odds with everything I've brought you through already. When it happens, don't be scared to tell them to sit down and be quiet. I'm doing a very specific thing here and I want you to remain true to everything I have put in you. And here's some news for you: what I'm doing isn't just about healing individuals; through this place I want to bring healing to entire nations. This nation and the nations of the world."

"Now, about the money. It might come in huge cheques or it might come in copper pennies but you will want for nothing. Don't skimp on anything that you do because you need the best for me and my house. The best carpets, the best curtains, the best chairs... even the best teacups. Don't be tempted to use that age-old excuse, 'We can't afford it.' I'm telling you to buy the best to honour me. The good news is that buying the best doesn't just

> make me happy – you'll get to dine like kings with the very best of food and drink. Tables laden with all kinds of good things glorifies me because people will walk in and say, 'Hallelujah! Hasn't the Lord done great things here?'"

The gleeful excitement when the people at Hollybush received that prophesy was almost tangible: "No one could contain their excitement that night. How powerfully and wonderfully God was at work, and what a promising future lay ahead of us. People coming from every direction to minister to us and to be ministered to. And who knew what else? It seemed absolutely anything was possible here in this place; there was just no end to what the Lord might do. Glory! We were really flowing in the Spirit and nothing could stop us or hold us back."

And it's a word of prophecy that is constantly on their lips. Frequently I've heard Jim and others say, "Well the original prophecy said such and such." Or, "That's what the prophecy meant – people coming from the North, South, East and West..." Or, "Yes, that makes senses – people coming in and going out...".

The story of Hollybush Farm and Fellowship is deeply tied to the lives of the Wilkinson family; for many years Jim and Cynthia but increasingly Joanna and Gabriella. The story of what has happened and is happening at Hollybush is the story of a Yorkshire farming family. When you arrive at the farm, you'll as likely find Jim talking about the best time to bale hay as praying. It's a story of God's Holy Spirit mixed in with livestock, crops, tractors and barns.

But if you want to know Jim's heart, there's no better sentence than one of the first written in *Miracle Valley.* "My long-standing association with the ministry that goes on at Hollybush Farm is one I deeply cherish." I am convinced that Jim has never seen what goes on at Hollybush as 'his' ministry or 'his' accomplishments. He merely got on board with what God was doing at the time and still tries to do the same.

Hollybush is unique in many ways. To a stranger, their Friday night meeting can seem like a bit of a circus. Some of these people are proper bouncing-off-the-walls Pentecostals. It would be very easy to write the lot of them off as 'crazy charismatics.' Half way through the worship, Gerhard will often pull out his shofar (ram's horn) and blow it at the four corners of the room. There used to be a woman called Rita who's gone to glory now. You could set your watch by her standing up and praying in tongues. And when I say praying, I mean shouting. There are a few flag wavers and if you look towards the front at the right hand side, you'll find half a dozen people dancing the Pentecostal Two-Step.

One woman described herself to me as the most reluctant member of Hollybush ever: "I didn't want to be like them. These people were all so rude – foreigners [people speaking in tongues] all praying at the same time, waving their hands in the air... And the women didn't even wear hats to church! I certainly didn't want to be one of them!"

But like lots of others who have a story about Hollybush, she was baptised in the Holy Spirit and then a few weeks later was baptised in the ice cold River Wiske that runs along the boundary of the farm. And then she started to experience for herself the stories of healings of the body and mind, of demons cast out, of coincidences that could only be explained by the intervention of God's Holy Spirit and about the faithfulness of a powerful God at Hollybush farm. They had visits from angels, saw the dead raised, were anointed with gold from heaven and saw answers to prayer beyond their wildest dreams.

Yet here's the paradox of Hollybush: somehow when you show up, God shows up. Perhaps you're there to expose it as a drug-fuelled cult, to laugh at the crazies or to sell something. Maybe your wife has emotionally blackmailed you into being there or it's an unintended stopping point on the way as you're hitch hiking to

London. Yes, I've heard every single one of those as a reason for showing up at Hollybush Farm. But every single one of those people told me the same thing: whenever they showed up, God showed up.

Hollybush is what it is: fully of broken and hurting people who don't have their stuff all together. People who are slightly eccentric and more than a little enthusiastic in the way they worship. But they're people who have seen the Holy Spirit doing things that sound incredible to the rest of us. They've seen just a little of the amazing power and love of a God who is still involved in the world and cares deeply about everything that we're going through.

So please read the story of Hollybush with an open mind; you don't have to wave your arms in the air or shout, 'Hallelujah!' but we invite you to listen for the Holy Spirit's prompting in your life. If you have any questions or we can pray for you in any way, please do get in touch.

ROOTS: FAITH, FAMILY, FARMING

There were certainly many folk in the little village of Snape, where I was brought up, who would vouch that I was a hopeless case. 'Jim Wilkinson?' I could imagine them saying. 'Why, we never knew such a little terror.' Though, if they were fair, they'd admit that I wasn't alone in the pranks I played on them. It took more than one mischievous youngster to stuff a chicken down someone's smoking chimney, or to roll a five-gallon drum of water to someone's door, leaning it so that the water would flood into the hall when the door was opened. Jim was a hopeless case, all right. With such a reputation I suppose it was understandable that a wave of relief swept the community along with the news that at 14 years of age I'd been converted.

It happened in the summer of 1944 when a jolly, silver-haired evangelist by the name of Reverend Tom Butler came to take a week's mission at the little Methodist chapel where I went each week with Mother and Dad and my brothers, Alan and Derek. Perhaps the villagers took this as their chance to see the little terror reformed and prayed extra hard that week. Or maybe it was the result of years of prayers from Mum and Dad and the folks at the chapel that I'd follow them in committing my life to the Lord.

Either way, on the Friday of that week I was one of the first out of my seat when the Reverend Butler invited us to step to the front if we wanted to receive Jesus as our Saviour. Unfortunately for the victims of those pranks, however, this 'conversion' was short-lived. I'd meant it at the time, of

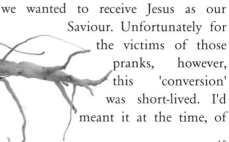

course, but looking back I think the decision to become a Christian had come from my head and not my heart. So there was no real change, except that I now had a different sort of reputation to live up to and my practical joking had to be rather more discreet.

Outwardly, though, the signs must have encouraged them. In order to keep up the pretence of having been 'born again,' I became increasingly involved with chapel activities, particularly the weekly Methodist Guild youth meetings, and I even joined one of the Mission Bands that went out on alternate Sunday evenings to take services at other chapels in our Methodist circuit. I thoroughly enjoyed these outings, and so bold did I become (or perhaps I'd even begun to believe that I was a Christian) that on many Sundays I was the one asked to deliver the sermon. But these sermons were never my own; I'd stumbled on a useful supply of sermon outlines in a Christian periodical, and with someone else's thoughts and interpretations to hand I would hold forth from the pulpit like a seasoned preacher.

The trouble was, just as the words were another man's, so was the conviction behind them. Yet no one ever challenged me about this - until one crisp November evening in 1948. We were on our way home from Ellingstring, a little village that sits tucked under the hill on the edge of Wensleydale. As so many times before, we'd taken the service in the little tin chapel that sits high off the road in the village street, and we'd enjoyed a good supper in the home of one of the chapel-goers. Now we were bowling home in the car, spinning through the twisty country lanes and laughing together at the memory of our host's face as we'd devoured every scrap of food laid before us.

But then, for me, the mood changed. As the laughs ran out and we began to motor down through the farms of High Ellington, the five of us in the car fell silent. And it was in that pause, just as we rounded a bend between the high hedges and dry-stone walls, that I heard the voice, 'You've been preaching about me tonight, haven't you?' I was seated in the middle of the back seat and glanced first to my left, but it wasn't Lilian Donaldson speaking to me. Then to my right, but my cousin Carl was looking the other way. Leonard Abel was at the wheel; perhaps they were his words? But Leonard was concentrating on keeping his Dad's little Ford Eight on the road.

And then it dawned on me. It must be the Lord! I'd never realised that God might sometimes speak to us with an audible voice - audible to me, anyway, if not to those around me - and all at once that sure knowledge brought a leap to my heart. Then, sitting there bumping along on that back seat, I thought I'd better answer the question. 'Mmmm,' I said. Almost immediately the clear, gentle voice came again. 'Do you really know me?' I had plenty of time to think on that. It was only another six miles to Snape, but on that brisk winter's night it seemed more like 60.

There had been a piercing challenge about that second question and in my heart there was a sense of urgency about answering it; urgency and, well, trepidation. Because in a flash I realised I'd been found out. God had known my heart all along. I didn't speak another word on that journey. When at last we reached the shadowy chapel in Snape I muttered a speedy, 'Cheerio,' and vanished into the night, charging off down the fields to our farm as though my tail was on fire. 'Do you really know me?' Soon the house loomed up in the darkness; no lights on and everyone in bed. I raced across the yard and into the kitchen, my heart pounding with the answer I knew I had to give. Up the stairs, into my room, and down on to my knees... "Lord, if that's you speaking to me - yes, please! I really want to know you."

It's a story that Jim loves to tell - I've read it in Miracle Valley, heard it preached from the pulpit and listened to it from Jim's mouth as we sat looking out over the land. The story of Jim's conversion is the start of the story of Hollybush.

In spite of Jim's decision at the age of 14, his involvement in the Methodist Guild, the

Mission Bands and chapel activities he had somehow missed the central truth. It's a mistake he's not going to make again. When asked what the one message that he wants this book to communicate, without hesitation, he replied, "Jesus Christ, the same yesterday, today and forever. He's alive. Get to know him. Make sure you know the Lord. Make sure that he's your best friend and keep him that way, because there's nobody else will touch him. I've known it since the eleventh of November, 1948..." As he's talking, he even gives the armrest of his rocking chair a couple of thumps with his fist like he does when he's preaching!

Of course, that was only the start for Jim. Just like John Wesley's "heart was strangely warmed," over 200 years earlier, in Jim's heart, "a strange and exciting fire was starting to burn." That Winter (of 1948), the Yorkshire Dales lay in a deep bed of snow but Jim was ministering with a new fervour – he wanted everyone else to have a piece of what he had. Instead of preaching other people's sermons, Jim preached his own sermons at the Mission Band services and he was never shy in making an appeal for people to give their lives to God.

In the midst of this, Jim's first experience of healing came quite unexpectedly. At the age of 19, Jim was visiting the optician for an eye-test. Wearing glasses had been necessary since he was six years old and had gone over the handlebars of his bike on his way home from school one summer's afternoon. As usual he had been rushing to reach the farm in time to join his dad on the evening milk round in Aiskew and Bedale. But on this night, Mr. Wilkinson senior went alone: Jim's tumble ended with a smashed brow-bone. In time, of course, the bone healed, but he was left with faulty vision in the bruised eye and on top of that was to suffer occasional severe migraines. Jim was told that he would always need spectacles but this time, when he went for the eye-test, something had changed.

"You've 20/20 vision," the surprised optician informed Jim. "Your problem seems to have cleared up naturally."

Naturally or supernaturally? In Jim's mind there was no doubt that the correction of his vision was one of the wonderful bonuses of the work of God in his life. The migraines still bothered him from time to time, but his eyesight was perfect. Never feeling at ease with spectacles, he got a real kick out of throwing them away. Released from the self-consciousness of the spectacles, Jim was now bolder than ever in his efforts to win others for the Lord.

Whatever the occasion, if it presented an opportunity for people to receive Christ, Jim was there in the thick of it: street evangelism, home visitation, Guild rallies, summer barbecues, special evangelistic outreaches – there was always something going on, always a fresh opening for the Gospel and as a result many people gave their lives to the Lord.

In spite of all the activity, Jim was frustrated that his own church wasn't doing enough. One of the young people from the church had been converted at an evangelistic campaign in Topcliffe and it bothered Jim that a church member had to go to another church to find the Lord. Jim and Rev. C.R. Ransome plotted and put the matter before the church and within a year, the Bedale Methodist Circuit held its own campaign – a week long effort that saw more than 70 people commit their lives to the Lord.

For Jim, the Rev. Ransome raised as many questions as he answered. As good Methodists, Jim and the rest of the congregation at Snape had been warned off the Pentecostals. They weren't like other Christians, they were told – speaking in strange babbling languages, they couldn't worship the Lord without making a lot of noise. What's more, they believed in a very dubious doctrine called 'the baptism in the Holy Spirit,' which any self-respecting Christian would steer well clear of. In short, they were weak people who needed an 'experience' - something extra to keep them going. Every time Jim heard this he would nod his head in hearty agreement. How little he knew what was coming through the character of George Breckon!

Jim didn't need anything added to his Christianity. He was soundly born again, had his Bible, was eager in prayer - and what's more was a good Wesleyan. He was totally secure and satisfied in his faith. But then there was Rev. Ransome. He had returned from missionary service in Nigeria shortly after the war and had come into the circuit as a breath of fresh air. He was a small, slight man with a bubbly, infectious laugh and bright, almost blazing eyes. In some indefinable way he always seemed larger than life. There was an energy about him, a spiritual energy that brought a new and exciting dimension to Bible studies and a dramatic lift to the preaching of the Gospel. When Rev. Ransome was taking a service there were few empty seats. From time to time he would relate his experiences in Africa, and he had some amazing stories to tell: stories of African Christians suddenly bursting forth in unknown languages as they worked away in the bush.

Some, he said, would fall flat on their faces and lie there in the dust, weeping non-stop for hours on end in the heat of the day. Then there would be times when these same Christians would be filled with a great joy, a joy that would come upon them as suddenly as the weeping, sweeping through their community in great waves of laughter.

"And what was the cause of this astonishing behaviour?" Rev. Ransome would ask us from the pulpit. "Why, it was the movement of the blessed Holy Spirit as He fell upon those people, moving them first to a great intercession as they wept for the work of God to be released upon their people, and then filling them with an overflowing joy as they received the assurance that God was indeed moving sovereignly upon their land in a great outpouring of His love and power. Indeed, it could have been nothing but a sovereign work of God," Rev. Ransome assured us, because what was happening was way beyond the experience of the missionaries working there, and in an incredible about-turn situation the white Christian workers found themselves learning about the Holy Spirit from their African converts.

"It was revival, of course," beamed the Reverend, "and in revival you are very aware of God's sovereignty. Why He chose to move upon our African brothers first only He knows, but it was nine months before He touched us missionaries in the same way; nine months before we too were baptised in the Spirit." He talked too about 'the gifts of the Spirit,' about 'miracles of healing,' and about other 'divine acts.' He even had some little booklets which explained such things, and these Jim read, partly out of curiosity and partly with disbelief - but mostly in confusion. As he worked on the farm or walked the cattle to Masham market on a Tuesday, Jim would turn these things over in his mind.

How was it that Methodists were told to keep away from Pentecostals and yet Rev. Ransome was preaching with great conviction about this strange 'baptism in the Spirit?' Perhaps it was all right for Africans, Jim told himself. After all, they needed an extra something to brighten up their spartan village life. And perhaps it was hardly surprising if some of that Holy Spirit stuff had rubbed off on the missionaries working with them. No one would blame Rev. Ransome for getting excited. Strange things might happen to anyone who ventured into a strange country, particularly if they stayed out in the sun too long. Besides, everyone knew that missionaries were... well, different.

"Probably it would be all right as long as he didn't start suggesting that we too needed this mystical 'baptism' experience," thought Jim. But one nagging question remained: what if the baptism was the key to that indefinable yet undeniable quality that somehow set this man apart from everyone else Jim knew? And as he pondered this he found myself wishing he'd known the Rev. Ransome who had set sail for Africa those many years ago – the green young Methodist missionary who probably hadn't had a good word to say for those crazy Pentecostals.

As the months and years passed, however, Jim thought less and less of these things. It seemed there were no easy answers to such grey areas of

Christian experience and it was best to get on with what he knew and loved best: preaching the Gospel. Yet it was while doing just that - out with the Mission Band one Sunday evening - that God began the foundational work of providing Jim with His own answers to those questions. One of the grey areas for him was healing. Did God heal today in the same miraculous way as did Jesus in the Gospels? It seemed unlikely. Yet at the same time Rev. Ransome's stories of healing miracles in Nigeria refused to go away, and Jim was also becoming more bold in his own faith, declaring that if God's Word said it, he believed it.

Shortly before Christmas, 1953, a group of us had been up to the little chapel at Langthome just beyond Bedale to take the evening service, and at the close of the meeting we were invited home for supper by a local farmer, Mr William Thompson. Still as eager as ever to help clear other people's dining tables, we accepted, unaware of what awaited us. Propped up in bed in the living room was Mrs Thompson. We learned that she was due to enter hospital for a hysterectomy - in those days a very serious operation. She was expected to spend 3 weeks in hospital and another five months convalescing. Several of us felt that we should pray with her for a successful operation and speedy recovery and agreed that we would pray a prayer of faith. Exactly how much faith we were able to muster I'm not quite sure because we insisted that Mrs Thompson's husband and two sons also be in on the prayer, probably so that there were plenty of us to share the blame if our faith didn't work. To our astonishment Mrs Thompson returned home after only two weeks in hospital, and within another couple of weeks she was up and about, easing herself back into the busy farmhouse routine. Perhaps secretly some of us were waiting for the backlash of this unusual recovery - would she have a relapse? But it never came. Her good health continued well into her eighties, having ailed hardly a thing since that memorable Christmas Sunday.

The following spring we were moved to put the prayer of faith into action again, this time in order to save a wedding and hoped-for honeymoon. On 6 May, 1954, my cousin Lorne was due to be married to Mary Lowes, a girl who'd been evacuated with her mother to our farm at the beginning of the war and whose family had settled in the area once peace had returned, But a few days before the big event, Mary began to feel unwell. By the Wednesday, the day before the wedding, she had turned yellow, been consigned to bed, and told by the doctor not to move. The diagnosis was yellow jaundice. She and Lome would have to postpone the happy day. But how could they notify all the guests in time? Few people had a telephone in those days. And what about the honeymoon? Two weeks booked and paid for and no refund possible. At a prayer meeting that evening we laid it before the Lord, asking and believing for a miracle. Again to my utter surprise, we got it. The following morning, as originally planned, Mary Lowes got out of bed, into her wedding dress and went and married her man. Her eyes were bright, her smile broad, and her skin the radiant pink of the blushing bride. I was as grateful as anyone but I was also intrigued. I was ready to pray for healing, even able now to believe that it would happen... but for God actually to act upon our faith in miracle-working power! Well, it needed some thinking about. And I hid these things in my heart, buried beneath the surface like the grain seeds lying in the soil of Hollins Farm.

What Jim's testimony of his early faith journey doesn't tell you is the story of growing up in Snape, a village of only about a hundred houses nestled between the North Yorkshire Dales and Moors and going to the village Methodist chapel.

The home I grew up in was a Christian one – mother and dad took me along to the little Methodist chapel in Snape and taught me how to pray. The chapel was a lively, evangelistic one and every week I was dressed in my Sunday-best for Sunday School. It was there that I learned the stories of our faith.

Snape was a very close knit village. Of course, it was war time and just after. Everybody had to work together because it was the only way you survived in war time – you had to watch each others' backs. Although it was the blackout, everybody pulled together. We had dog fights over our farm during the war because Leeming Aerodrome was just down the road and they were always trying to have a go at it. We used to stand there and watch them at 14 years old. The spitfires used to try and get behind them and push them back to the North Sea. We even had a searchlight battery on the farm and the lane was often full of munitions and gelignite.

As I look back now, why did everybody stick together? Because there was nowhere to go. The cinema at Bedale was two miles there and two miles back on the bike and if we wanted to go to Northallerton, that was ten miles each direction. When I was a teenager I was an operator in the cinema at Bedale. Very few people had a car, fewer people had two vehicles – it was still 'on yer bike' or a little Ford 8 if you were lucky. Looking back, the country was bankrupt – everybody was at square one at the same time. After the war, thank God there was no blackout – we could have lights on our cars again. We could have the blinds open.

The first year that I was at home, I ploughed 60 acres at just over 15 years of age. What tractor was I driving?Two horses! That first winter I ploughed with horses. We had four horses and you changed them at dinner time. I left school early in June rather than September to go and work on the farm. I did my school cert at the end of June and I left straight away. They wouldn't let us leave until we'd had the exams. My brothers were away; my elder brother was at another farm and my other brother was in the Fleet Air Arm somewhere in Japanese waters. So ploughing was my job for the first Winter, in amongst looking after the cattle and delivering milk twice a day, seven days a week until 1953 when the bottle came in. There's no rest for a dairy farmer!

In 1953 we quit making milk and selling it. Before that, you had to keep doing what you were doing because of the war but in 1953 you could do what you wanted rather than what you were told. We had to grow five acres of mangels [also known as mangelwurzels] that went down to what is now the sugar beet factory at York and they were made into jam; raspberry and strawberry jam. There was no raspberries or strawberries in them; it was all food colouring and the strawberry seeds were made out of balsa wood shavings left over from building aircraft!

Then we had to grow about 10 acres of flax for linseed for parachute silk. You had to pull it by hand to get the length of stem to get the length of flax. It all had to be pulled by the roots. There was a gang master who came with ten German prisoners of war from Northallerton prison. We could do an acre a day so it took 10 days. The German lads used to bring their own cook and the other chap was a soldier with a rifle but nobody attempted to escape. I mean where could you go to? And the cook was a very good cook, I'll tell you. So I got the benefit of that!

In 1956 the first tractor I bought was a little grey Fergie with a three furrow plough that cost me £535 with the plough. They are valuable now – you can still get two or three thousand for one. And the difference between the big tractor out there and the little grey Fergie was the Fergie could go all day, whatever you were doing, on about four gallons of fuel. Some of these big new ones use about ten gallons an hour I would think.

In 1953 things gradually got better when petrol rationing was finished. We still delivered milk twice a day every day until 1953 when the bottles came in and I was 23 years of age. We milked by hand at first but we got a milking machine in 1951. Even then it wouldn't always start – it ran on a little Lister stationary engine. We had no problems sleeping in those days!

It was a praying church [Snape Methodist Church]. A lot of young people my age group. There'd be about 60 young people at the same time between 14 and 20. There was a Guild which was on a Monday night. Then once a month in the Winter months on behalf of the Temperance Society we'd put on a village play.

The Methodist Guild, although now somewhat dis-established from the Methodist Church nationally still has a local presence in many churches, including (believe it or not) in the little village of Snape. Still only during the Winter months, though!

The Methodist church in Snape is still there,
"Showing, sharing and serving Jesus in the community."
Copyright © Ripon & Lower Dales Methodist Circuit.
Used with permission.

"The Wesley Guild (also known as WG or Methodist Guild) is a worldwide Christian organisation aimed to retain young people within the Wesleyan Church. It was founded on 30 July 1896 in Liverpool, England and its aim is to help young people to band together using the model known as four Cs (4Cs of Christ) that stands for the: Comradeship of young Methodists, Consecration of body, soul and spirit to the Lord Jesus Christ, Culture of mind to ensure thoughtful and intelligent life, and Christian Service for the building up of the Church and the Kingdom of God. These 4Cs are also reflected on Royal Blue and Gold Wesley Guild logo (cross-like logo) with the motto being 'One Heart, One Way'"[1]

At least that was all true when Jim joined the guild in the 1940s. Sadly, the Methodist Guild is no longer a youth organisation and these days caters to ageing men and women who still hark back to the glory days of the M.A.Y.C. London weekend, wearing their

1   http://en.wikipedia.org/wiki/Wesley_Guild

green and yellow and going to the Albert Hall for the annual Methodist Association of Youth Clubs rally. Don't be fooled by any of that though: an aging Methodist Guild plus the Holy Spirit could easily change the world.

Of course, as Jim wryly comments, the Methodist Guild served another purpose in the community. The other big youth organisation in rural communities was (and is) the Young Farmers Club. If a bachelor farmer hoped to find a bride, then Young Farmers Club socials and Methodist Guild rallies were often rich pickings; and Christian parents hoped and prayed that their daughters would find their husbands at the Guild since the Young Farmers Clubs often had a reputation for their wild ways. And it was in the Guild that Jim and Cynthia met.

I'd met a slim blonde girl called Cynthia Biker casually through the Methodist Guild up at Leyburn and I'd got to know that she had a very fine gift for singing. An exceptional gilt, in fact. Her talent had first come to light as a ten-year-old in the local Methodist choir. From there her mother had encouraged her into singing lessons and, later, the local operatic society. By the time she was 16 she was singing the soprano part in all the oratorios - Creation, Eljiah, Isaiah. The prediction was that she was destined for great things. But my thoughts had been different; I wasn't too interested in worldly success. I was hoping Cynthia would give her life to the Lord so that she could use that wonderful voice for Him. Now she had, and she could. But I could not have known that a storm was about to break.

Cynthia became a Christian during a trip to Kelvin Hall in Glasgow to hear Billy Graham. That was in April and in September of that year Cynthia was due to leave the Dales to enrol at the Royal Academy of Music in London - and at no charge. The tutor who had interviewed her was so confident of her potential to be a top-flight operatic star that he had taken her on as his own personal student.

But two weeks after committing her life to Christ, Cynthia backed out of the Academy, gave up her singing lessons, and calmly told her parents that from now on she was going to sing only for the Lord. The storm broke. Her parents exploded. Her tutor tore up her music and threw it in her face. "Get out!" he fumed. "GET OUT!" When the dust had settled her mother tried to reason with her, but Cynthia was adamant. Not because of any conversion whim, but because God's love had won her heart and she had felt impressed deep in her spirit that this was what He was asking her to do. It wasn't so much a case of giving up her gift, she tried to explain, but of dedicating it to the Lord.

To the delight of so many in the local churches, that is exactly what she did. She committed her singing ability to Christ's service, accepting every opportunity that came her way to sing for His glory. To me this was wonderful. We were short of good singers in our Mission Bands and now I had someone top-rate I could call upon when I was invited to take a church service; someone through whose music the Lord really spoke. Many times when Cynthia was singing the Holy Spirit would move upon a church and there wouldn't be a dry eye in the house. That sort of singing ministry was a God-send to anyone who had to follow it with the preaching of the Gospel.

But the one person I had not expected God to speak to while Cynthia was singing was myself. And He did it once again in that unforgettable, audible voice. It happened at a little church in the village of Warsill, about 20 miles from Snape. Cynthia was up front, her beautiful voice filling that building with praise as I sat in my pew ready to get up and give the Gospel address. It was then that the Lord spoke. "That's the girl I've got for you." For a moment I was stunned. Had I heard right? But really there was no doubt. That voice - the same gentle voice that had brought me into a living relationship with the Lord seven years earlier - had been unmistakable. And the message, even in the midst of Cynthia's singing, had been as clear as the texts hanging on the church wall. God was at work in my life, directing me in terms that I could not fail to understand. There wasn't a shadow of doubt in my mind as to what my heavenly Father was saying: "Jim, my plan is for you and Cynthia to be married."

Sprung upon me so suddenly this was a bit daunting, and perhaps the natural man would have tended to panic. I could think of several reasons why such a suggestion was not on. For a start, sitting beside me in the pew was Mary Wilson, my girlfriend of two years and a lass of whom I was very fond. Our parents would have put it in stronger terms than that and already had us married off. Only the announcement of the engagement was preventing them from making plans.

To further complicate matters, Cynthia had a boyfriend. Perhaps he had his own thoughts about whom Cynthia should marry. And to cap it all, the prospect of calling at Cynthia's house did not exactly excite me. Her mother, having come to the conclusion that Cynthia had been brainwashed, blamed, "that Jim Wilkinson." If it wasn't for him and his extreme religion her girl would be on her way to the top of the operatic world. In short, Jim had smashed her dreams. There was no way she was going to let me have her daughter's hand as well. But all that reasoning left God out and I had been a Christian long enough to know that the Lord does not make mistakes.

Furthermore I had learned that His design for my life was born out of His love for me: if He asked me to do anything I could be sure that I'd be blessed in doing it. And I'd learned to trust Him. He had never yet asked me to do anything without also showing me how to go about it, and I knew that in this situation too - prickly though it might be - He had already worked out the details. My part was simply to obey.

I didn't waste any time in setting things in motion. Something else He had taught me over the years was that His timing is always perfect: He was never early, never late. He always brought His word at the precise moment of His sovereign choosing. So who was I to delay?

Even so, I knew that the first step wouldn't be easy, and as I pulled the car to a halt outside Mary's home later that night I felt a little tremble in the pit of my stomach.

"I've something to tell you," I said, switching off the engine. Then a voice from somewhere - an alien voice - tried to tell me I was being very foolish. Why throw away two good years of happy relationship? Stick with Mary. But I'd learned to recognise the enemy's voice too, and I pressed ahead. Taking hold of Mary's hand, as though that would soften the blow, I went on: "The Lord spoke to me tonight, Mary. I - I believe He wants us to part."

She glanced at me, a sudden pain in her eyes, then turned away. "What makes you say that?"

I tried as best I could to explain about Cynthia and the voice. "It's not that I have any feelings for her, you understand. She's a lovely girl, I know, but I'd not thought of her in the same way as I've thought of you. We've had some good times together, you and I, but... well, what can I say? I just know the Lord has spoken."

I didn't want to hurt Mary, I really didn't, and all at once I knew that God had taken care of that too. There was a touch of moisture in her eyes but her lips were smiling as she said: "Can we pray about it? I want to be as sure about it as you are, Jim. But - if that's what the Lord wants, that's what He'll have."

Our parents were less understanding, but of course at first we couldn't divulge exactly why we'd broken up - not until I'd told Cynthia. At that point I realised how much simpler it would have been if the Lord had told her of His plans, too. But He hadn't. Yet the Spirit was at work preparing her, for already she had begun to realise that the relationship with her boyfriend - a non-Christian - was not what God wanted for her. At the same time Jim Wilkinson was asking her for a date. Could this be the Lord? I assured her that it was; that God had spoken very clearly to me about it. But she was not so sure. Anyone could manipulate events to their advantage by claiming that "God told me..."

For a while she was very cautious of me. Gradually, though, the boyfriend was phased out and Jim was phased in. Another hurdle over.

But then there was Mother. As I'd guessed, the news that I was now dating her daughter did not endear me to Mrs Biker. It was bad enough that this religious maniac had lured her girl into accepting his fanatical beliefs – a scandal roundly condemned by her own minister, no less – but actually to have the man calling at the house was an outrage. She did her best to discourage me. Often I would call for Cynthia only to be told, "She's not in. She's gone for a ride up the Dale with friends." While all the time Cynthia would be in the house, unaware that I was on the doorstep.

Eventually love won through, a love the Lord had given me both for Cynthia and her parents. When, a year later, we told them that we wanted to get engaged, they grudgingly agreed. Things were eased still further a few weeks later when our parents met for the first time and took a liking to each other.

The timing of the wedding, set for the summer of 1957, fitted in well with Dad's plans for getting the last of his children off his hands. My brother Alan and his wife Joyce had a farm at Rainton, Derek (married to Vera) was well into his chosen career as a draughtsman with Durham County Council and now, after a good deal of searching, Dad had found a small farm for his youngest boy at Sandhutton, an old village perched at the northern tip of the beautiful Vale of York.

It was an arable farm of 76 acres known as The Limes, and it had come up for sale under rather sad circumstances. The vendor, a Mrs Fawell, had lost her husband after a long illness shortly before the war and since then she had been trying to keep the farm going with the help of a daughter and hired help. For a long time now it had been an uphill struggle and at last she had decided to sell up. We heard about the sale before the farm came on to the market thanks to Derek Alsop, one of Dad's friends and an auctioneer in the market town of Northallerton. "It might be just what you're looking for," Mr Alsop had told Dad on the phone. "A nice little place. Needs a bit doing to it, but the potential's good."

We drove down to Sandhutton after tea that evening and saw the property for ourselves. It was exactly as the auctioneer had said. The Limes was a farm of manageable size for a young man starting out on his own, and considering Mrs Fawell's circumstances it wasn't in too bad a condition. Some of the buildings were derelict and would have to be replaced, and the place was badly in need of some concrete working areas around the barns, but those things were incidental.

What mattered was the condition of the soil and Mr Alsop had thought it promising, After calling at the house, Dad and I walked out over the land, feeling the give of the earth beneath our boots. Dad was more expert at this than I, of course, but even with my limited experience I could tell that we were treading on good soil. If your foot barely makes an impression there's too much clay; if it sinks in too far the soil's too light. But the earth here felt right. Out in the middle of the field Dad bent down and scooped up some soil in his big work-gnarled hands, at first feeling the body in it and then letting it sift through his fingers.

His craggy, weather- tanned face, at first thoughtful, cracked into a smile. "That's good stuff," he declared. "That'll serve you well, son."

I nodded, pleased. "There's a lot to be done," I said, pointing to fields beyond that were overrun with couch grass. "But if the soil's all right..."

"Aye. You could really make something of this little place."

"What about the house?" I asked as we walked back up through the tumbledown farm buildings. "That'll need some work on it too."

"A bit of renovation," Dad agreed. He stopped in the yard, pushed back his cap and stood looking up at the great bulk of the old farmhouse. "If I were you I'd divide the place in two, then you could let the other half to one of your men. It's much bigger than you'll need, anyway." It was a good idea; the rent from sub-letting would help with the overall rent I would be paying Dad for the farm.

We went into the house and had a further talk with Mrs Fawell, and then Dad drew me aside. "You think it would suit you, then?"

"It's ideal," I replied. "An answer to prayer. Cynthia's going to love it."

We took possession of The Limes in April 1956 and it was then that Dad officially pushed me out of the nest. "From now on you're on your own, son," he told me as he handed me the keys to the new farm - which may sound brutal but really was the best thing a father could have done for his son. And there was more to come. One of Dad's insurance policies had recently matured and he said he wanted me to have the money. "It'll help you get started," he explained, as though he hadn't done enough for me already. The cheque was for £599 - in those days a great deal of money; enough to buy the best tractor on the market. Over the next year or so I spent many long hours over at Sandhutton carrying out the alterations to the farmhouse and decorating right through. By June, 1957, the place was ready for Mr and Mrs Jim Wilkinson.

But before our own happy day Cynthia and I were pleased to hear of another couple's wedding. The groom was an old pal, Leonard Abel, and walking up the aisle on his arm that glorious July day was someone I was glad to know was so happy - my old flame, Mary Wilson. They were well suited, I knew that, and I was so thankful for God's leading in this all-important matter of choosing a life partner. For I was aware that when the Lord had spoken to me so clearly that Sunday evening He had not only released me to marry Cynthia, but He'd also released Mary to marry Len. Their marriage was important too, and I was grateful that day for the reminder God gave me that in His sovereign will He has a plan for each of us; that to Him, everyone is special.

Our own wedding took place a week later on the 25th of July 1957, but this time the sun was not in attendance. Cynthia walked to the chapel from her nearby home in pouring rain, her father holding the umbrella and we had to be thankful that the downpour let up long enough for the wedding photos to be taken. But nothing could dampen the joy of knowing that we had been married in the Lord, and crossing the threshold of The Limes later that day for the first time as man and wife we were very aware that if our marriage was to be blessed it had to be a threesome: the two of us, plus Jesus.

Likewise with the farm. So, during that first week in our new home, we knelt together and asked the Lord to take us into partnership with Him there at The Limes. We also agreed that we wouldn't plan any children for seven years: that those first years of our marriage partnership would be the Lord's. "Father," I prayed, "we dedicate our marriage, our home, our work to your service. Whatever you want for us, that's what we want. We are totally open to everything you wish for our lives." I didn't realise it at the time, but it was a dangerous prayer to pray, and one which at a future date I would be tempted to regret. Was I really willing to accept everything God wanted me to have?

For 60 years, God has taken Jim and Cynthia at their word – their marriage, home and work were indeed dedicated to His service and they are still open to and waiting for everything that God has for them.

And the answer to the one question that nobody's brave enough to ask? Jim and Cynthia have never taken a penny of salary from the church finances. The farm by some miracle has brought in enough to support not just the Wilkinsons but almost always three other families at the same time too.

SHOOTS

One of this part of Yorkshire's most famous exports is Wensleydale cheese. Locals will tell you that it goes especially well with fruit cake. Wensleydale cheese has a history stretching back to 1150 AD when it was made by the Cistercian monks. In 1935, Kit Calvert (the general manager) managed to negotiate a management buyout of the heavily indebted dairy and all during the industrial depression of the 1930s. His name is now spoken of reverentially in the Dales as the man who saved Wensleydale cheese. And there would be no Wallace and Gromit without their famous cheese! The Wensleydale Creamery is still producing cheese in the village of Masham (don't pronounce the 'h' if you don't want to sound like a tourist – it's Mass-am to the locals). You can even take a tour of the creamery and try out dozens of different varieties.

Kit Calvert wasn't just a cheese-man though. In 1952, Jim was involved in forming the Wensleydale Evangelistic Crusade along with two other men: local farmer Alf Suttill and Kit Calvert. Under this banner, the three men held weekly outreach meetings in the near-redundant Congregational Church in Leyburn and also launching out to take regular open-air services in many of the little villages up and down the Dales.

It was off the back of the Wensleydale Evangelistic Crusade that Jim and others began to get involved in the Billy Graham Evangelistic Association.

Billy Graham (now well into his 90s) rose to celebrity status in the early 1950s as an international evangelist, having cut his teeth as the first full time worker for Youth For Christ. One rather reserved television news report from the time begins with some beautiful footage of a famous London landmark:

"Westminster Abbey. For a thousand years, Britain's link between church and state. Here beneath its towering Gothic piers and vaults, England's kings and queens from the time of William the Conqueror have been crowned. It's towers and transepts rising above Parliament Square to mark with magnificence the place of coronation. With most churches only sparsely attended and with Christian leadership tremendously concerned for the fate of the nation, a committee of the clergy and laymen invited an American evangelist to come and lead them in a spiritual crusade: a crusade to restore the faith of our fathers. It was the week before the crusade started that Mr. and Mrs. Graham disembarked at Southampton, continuing by train to Waterloo Station in London. To at least one station official, this was the biggest welcome in 40 years at Waterloo Station. [Choir singing on the station platform in the background]"[2]

Another much more enthusiastic voice-over for a different piece includes some footage of Billy Graham preaching. It's worth remembering this was still only 1954, shortly after most people had purchased their televisions so that they could watch the coronation.

The mighty Haringay Arena in London draws a capacity crowd of over 11,000 for the first meeting in Britain of the American evangelist [sic] team headed by Billy Graham. Graham, who wears a slate grey suit and a modest tie makes his address from a purple draped platform.

"I'm not going to deliver my message now but just to say a word of greeting to you that are here tonight. We're delighted tonight to have these newspaper people here. It's been a long time. Perhaps you can see them [applause]. It's been a long time since evangelism and revival and Christ and God was front page news around the world and we thank God for it."

---

2   https://www.youtube.com/watch?v=VD_VqeX79-o

Billy Graham's unorthodox methods may not be to all tastes but he and his team backed by a choir of nearly 2,000 voices believe they will fill Haringay each night during their three month crusade in London.[3] [Choir sings in background: "Guide me, O Thou great Redeemer / Pilgrim through this barren land / I am weak but Thou art mighty / Hold me with Thy powerful hand / Bread of heaven, bread of heaven / Feed me till I want no more / Feed me till I want no more."[4]

With such a wonderful opportunity happening on his 'doorstep' (216 miles door-to-door from The Limes at Sandhutton to the Harringay Arena in North London, or a 432 mile round trip), Jim was in with both feet: there were coach trips to London to be arranged, prayer meetings to attend and homes to visit with invitations to the crusade. For weeks beforehand there wasn't a moment to spare, and Jim was in his element, helping to make a way for folk to hear the great evangelist, and hopefully to commit their lives to Christ.

Two years later, it all happened again at Kelvin Hall in Glasgow (almost 30 miles closer to home!). Jim remembers one trip to Glasgow in particular with fondness because it was then that Cynthia gave her life to Christ.

Cynthia decided that she would be home-maker (not just a housewife) and so her energies were spent making the farmhouse at Sandhutton comfortable and inviting. "I want it to be a place where people will be happy to come," she told Jim. "A place where people can meet the Lord... where the Lord Himself will feel at home."

Jim and Cynthia had started attending the Methodist chapel at Sandhutton and word spread amongst the young people that there was an 'open house' at The Limes. The adults weren't so keen

3   http://www.britishpathe.com/video/billy-graham-starts-crusade
4   Guide Me, O Thou Great Jehovah by William Williams, 1745, Public domain

because they had heard about Jim and his 'fanatical religion.' However, it wasn't long before the minister asked the Wilkinsons to take on the youth work – the Wednesday night Guild meeting. And it was at The Limes that Jim and Cynthia began an informal fellowship meeting in their home on Friday evenings.

That fellowship meeting was quickly to become the highlight of the week not just for Jim and Cynthia but for the little group of faithful souls who began to come along.

George Breckon was a local man and like Jim, was from Yorkshire farming stock who could trace his farming ancestors back to the sixteenth century. His family had always owned the same rambling little farmhouse, Duck House, over in Farndale. The farmhouse has been there for so long, it is a Grade II* listed building – it may well be the only surviving example of a Moors farmhouse of the post-medieval period.

The Wilkinsons and the Breckons knew one another not just through farming but also through some of the local prayer meetings around the area that they used to go to. George, like Jim was the next generation in a long line of Methodists. George married one of the Dobson sisters, a locally popular family of gospel singers who sang close harmony. The Dobson Family were often invited to local chapels at Harvest Thanksgiving and other special occasions. So Jim and Cynthia got to know the family and their 'roadie'. The family lived 'just over the hill' (Jim's words – by 'the hill' he meanss Sutton Bank, a steep one in four gradient that gets blocked over a hundred times a year by caravanners and ill-prepared motorists).

George took over the farm from his father in the 1940s but in 1961, George severely injured his back and was told by doctors that he was without hope; a physical write-off. They sent him home to bed where he spent much of the following two years. Only occasionally was he fit enough to work and even then he had to take care not to damage his back even further. The result was that the farm began to run down, his money ran out and his morale lay in pieces. In his own words, he was physically, financially, mentally and spiritually broke.

Until then George had had a fairly lively faith – converted at 17 and lay preaching at 19 – but now he felt totally abandoned by God. And yet his faith somehow managed to hang on. Each week he would listen in to Christian radio programmes in the hope that sooner or later someone would somehow throw him a lifeline. One of the programmes that intrigued him most was hosted by American evangelist and Bible teacher Oral Roberts. Almost every week Rev. Roberts made some mention of God's power to heal, and occasionally the preacher's wife would read out letters sent in by people testifying that they had experienced that healing for themselves. George wondered could God really heal as dramatically and miraculously today as did Jesus?

Before long, George had a chance to find out. Having spoken on 'How To Receive Faith For Healing,' Rev. Roberts said he would pray a prayer of faith which the listener could make his own. "If you desire to be healed," he went on, "may I encourage you to reach out in faith and lay your hand upon your radio set while I am praying." This wouldn't actually heal anyone, he pointed out, but it would most certainly help to release the listener's faith. A moment later Rev. Roberts began praying, and more in desperation than faith George reached out his hand. As he connected with the radio he felt a shock-wave flash up his arm and suddenly his whole body began shaking with a tremendous power. Healing power!

The very next night, George went to a prayer meeting in Pickering to give thanks. There were some Spirit-filled people there and they prayed for him. He got radically filled with the Holy Spirit.

Within two weeks George was back at work, lifting the heaviest loads and not even feeling a twinge. He had been completely healed. More than that, his life had been revolutionized. He returned to lay preaching with a fresh and burning zeal, he committed himself to studying his Bible with an excitement he'd never known, and in his prayer times he hungered after knowing more of the God who had so powerfully touched him. Sometimes his longing would be so great that he would spend days in prayer and fasting, determined to draw closer to the heart of God and to hear more clearly from Him.

One thing he had not expected to hear was the call that came to him in the summer of 1963 – the call to leave farming and to commit his time to preaching the Gospel. This took him by surprise because only recently had he moved from Duck House to a bigger farm down at Pickering. (God not only healed him but prospered his business, too!) Nevertheless the call was so clear and Gladys, his wife, agreed this was the way the Lord was leading. George immediately began making plans to sell up. By March of the following year it was all settled, and centuries of Breckons farming the Yorkshire hills had come to an end. From now on George would be planting a very different type of seed and looking for a very different type of crop.

He was a big man with a booming voice and bright, laughing eyes; a charismatic figure whose fiery preaching and flowing, swept-back hair put Jim in mind of another Methodist whose burning passion for souls had brought him to thunder out his Gospel message in these same hills hundreds of years before – the great John Wesley himself. Clearly George Breckon would be an asset to the outreach meetings, and Jim was delighted to learn that his association was not simply a preacher's whim. "The Lord," George explained, "has specifically told me to come and identify with the work you are doing." What an encouragement!

But before long a niggling little cloud was to drift into this promisingly bright picture. It was the summer of 1966. For many weeks George Breckon had been coming to the Friday night meetings and from the start he had been a great help, drawing on his vast Bible knowledge and deep understanding of the Scriptures to teach and build up the many young Christians who were now meeting regularly together. But now and then he would slip in certain things that Jim would be unhappy about. Certain things that weren't... well, they weren't Wesleyan!

At first I thought it best to ignore these little asides in the hope that nothing would come of them, rather than take issue with the man and blow the remarks out of proportion. That would only draw attention to what I saw as dubious doctrines. Best to say nowt and let them pass. But George wasn't letting anything pass; he was just getting warmed up. It came to a head one Friday tea-time. We'd invited George and Gladys for a meal prior to the evening's meeting and I could tell from the moment I opened the door that George was excited about something. It wasn't the first time I'd seen him like this – bright-eyed and beaming – but I'd never actually got around to asking him about it, perhaps because I was afraid of what the answer might be. But this time the words just slipped out – and I could have kicked myself.

"Jim! Cynthia! I've just got to tell you – there's something more!"

It was too late to back out now. "More than what?"

"More than what you've got. It's the Spirit. You need to be baptised in the Spirit. There's just so much more!"

My hackles spiked up. I'd known it was coming – for months I'd known it was coming – but still it grated. Maybe I could laugh it off. "You've got the wrong man, George. I don't need any new experience; I'm quite happy as I am, thank you. The only experience I'm interested in right now is Cynthia's chicken casserole. Come on in, it's all ready."

But George wouldn't be stopped. "You can be filled with the Spirit, Jim! You can know power in your life and in your preaching – enter into a new dimension of faith. And all you have to do is ask. Do it, Jim, do it – you'll get blessed more than you ever thought possible."

Instinctively I reached out for the stock answers. "I don't believe in all that stuff," I countered as we settled round the table. "The baptism in the Spirit isn't for today; it was a once-and-for-all experience at Pentecost – to get the Christian Church off the ground."

"But look at me," beamed George. "It happened to me and it changed my life."

"I received the Holy Spirit when I was born again," I protested. "It was part of the package. There isn't anything more – you're just fooling yourself, George." He gulped a mouthful of casserole.

"I know we receive the Spirit when we're born again, but that's just the beginning. There's a glorious infilling, too, and you need that before the gifts of the Spirit can be released in your life."

"But we've seen miracles," Cynthia piped up. "We know all about the work of the Holy Ghost."

"Aye, we've prayed for people and they've been healed," I said. "That's power."

"But that power came direct from God," argued George. "He wants you to receive power for yourself, so that you can use it in your own life, too. The Scripture promises it: "Ye shall receive power!" Acts 2."

"And I've preached on it. But that was just for the Early Church, George. The gifts petered out with Peter." The casserole disappeared and in came the strawberry shortcake. But it wasn't about to sweeten me up. In fact as the discussion bounced back and forth across the table I found myself becoming more and more irritated. Whatever I said, George seemed to have an answer for it and in the end I began clawing for an escape in the muck of personal remarks. First: "You're more emotional than I am, George. Maybe you needed some sort of experience to keep you

going. Me, I've got my feet firmly on the ground."
Then: "Let's face it, George, you were in a bad way
when God picked you up. He had to do something
pretty dramatic else you were a goner." And inevitably: "I
don't need your Pentecostal ideas. I'm a Methodist and
always have been. My father's faith has always been
good enough for me before and I don't see any
reason to add to it now." Unsettlingly, Oral
Roberts himself was a Methodist.

The meeting that evening did not go well – at
least, not for me. Our confrontation – for it seemed that was what
it was – had left a bad taste in my mouth, not least because I'd
been driven to realise I had no real answers to George's
enthusiasm – only prejudices. And though I wouldn't have
admitted it then, he had stirred up an ugly part of me that nearly
20 years of walking with the Lord had failed to touch. Pride. It
was an old enemy and perhaps my biggest, but because of its very
nature I would never own up to its presence in my life. And by
denying it I allowed it free rein. That night as Cynthia and I
climbed into bed I was still smarting from George's blundering
approach. Why had he brought this up now? From a comment in
one of the meetings I knew that it had been three years since he'd
received his so-called 'baptism in the Spirit', so why try foisting it
upon us now? I'd known his views for months, just as he must
have known mine. I'd thought, foolishly, that we had an
understanding. Certainly I was happy to work with George in
evangelism so long as he kept his peculiar ideas about the Holy
Spirit to himself. But now... well, now he'd rocked the boat.

To add insult to injury that night Cynthia would not agree with
me when I complained that George had ruined our meal together.
To my horror I discovered that she was not at all convinced that
George had got this business of the Holy Spirit quite wrong.
"Maybe there is something in what he says," she suggested,
snuggling down between the sheets.

"I doubt it," I snorted as I fumbled in my bedside cabinet for the indigestion tablets. "Take it from me, Cynthia, he's on a loser there. You wait and see."

She turned towards me, her eyes wide open again, and her words were like a spear to my heart. "But what about Reverend Ransome up at Snape? You remember you once told me about him and how he'd got this baptism thing when he was out in Africa. They can't both be wrong, him and George – can they?"

She'd hit a tender spot and I had to cover it fast. "It was spending all that time in the sun did that to him," I spluttered. "There's nothing in it, not really. Shall I turn this light out?"

But Cynthia did not look ready for sleep. Suddenly fully awake, she propped herself up on her elbows and looked squarely at me. "But if it is of the Lord – if there is something more..."

"Then the Lord will give it to us," I said, irritably. "We won't have to go asking and fussing about it; He'll just give it to us."

She fell back against the pillow and lay staring up at the ceiling, lost in her thoughts. I switched out the light and settled down to sleep, certain I'd escaped. But then Cynthia spoke again. "Do you remember that prayer we prayed when we first came here, love?"

"What about it?"

"I've never forgotten it," she murmured. "We said that we wanted whatever the Lord had in store for us – that we'd welcome everything He wanted to give us." In the darkness she couldn't see my anger.

Summer mellowed into autumn, autumn shivered into winter but George Breckon would not go away. As regularly and irritatingly as the migraines which continued to plague me, the man persisted in turning up for our Friday evening meetings and barely a week passed without him hounding us with talk about 'the baptism'. It was annoying. I liked George, but he was making life difficult for me. His persistence was irking me, robbing me of my joy, pushing my normally endless patience to the limit. Why wouldn't he give up? Take 'no' for an answer? Go and peddle his Pentecostal ideas elsewhere?

It would have been easier, of course, if others in the Friday group had found him overbearing – but no one did. They all loved him and apparently couldn't hear enough about his Spirit-baptised experiences. It was just me – and as host of the house meetings, as well as one of the longest-standing Christians in the group, I had to love him too. It was not easy.

Eventually I developed a defensive mechanism. When George came to tea (Cynthia would insist on inviting him) I brushed aside every reference to Pentecost or the gifts of the Spirit with either a little joke or a cutting wise-crack, depending on the degree of threat it posed. I was sure that if I laughed it off long enough George would lose heart and give me up as an impossible case. He didn't.

I tried another tack: monopolise the conversation. Talk about anything and everything – the new family at church, the price of breeding pigs, Joanna's latest antics – any subject to keep George off his hobby-horse. But occasionally I'd have to stop for a mouthful of food and before I could swallow George would leap in with, "Well, have you thought any more about..."

Where would it all end? I think from the very beginning George had never doubted where it would end and Cynthia was giving him every encouragement to believe he was going to see his goal achieved. It was very unsettling. While I was pulling further and further away from the likelihood of ever pursuing the things George spoke of, Cynthia was clearly edging nearer. From her early, 'If there is something more...' she had now moved on to, 'If God's in it, I want it.'

But how could it be of God, I reasoned, if it was driving us apart? (I didn't realise it then, but that's one of the devil's favourite lines.) On the surface of our relationship everything was fine – well, more or less, as long as I could pretend not to be rattled by George – but underneath I was seething. I was the spiritual head of our home – Cynthia ought to be taking her lead from me. All my arguments were sound – until they were examined closely. Then they were identified for what they were: cleverly disguised pride.

Occasionally these mental volcanoes would erupt and I would try to convince Cynthia that she was wrong; that she should close her mind to George's crazy ideas. But I should have known better. From the moment Cynthia had welcomed Christ into her life 12 years earlier she had pursued the things of God with a zeal that put even my enthusiasm in the shade. She had always meant business with the Lord – and there was no stopping her now. If the baptism in the Spirit was for real and it would enable her to receive more of God then Cynthia was going for it with arms wide open. Hers was an uncomplicated faith – and perhaps even naïve, I thought – but it always seemed to bring results.

It was no different this time. It happened the following spring at Valley Road Baptist Church in Northallerton. George was holding a week long mission there, taking a different theme each night. One evening it would be 'The Blood of Jesus', another 'The Christian Life' and so on. The last night, I discovered, he was to preach on 'The Baptism in the Holy Spirit'.

"You'll not get me along to that," I told Cynthia. "I have enough of that man trying to indoctrinate me here in my own home without hearing it from the pulpit."

"But you don't mind if I go, Jim?"

"For all the good it'll do you…"

Cynthia said no more about it and that night I stayed home to baby-sit while a friend drove her into town. Three hours later she was driven back again though she might just as easily have flown.

She was still walking on air when she came into the lounge. Never in my life had I seen someone so elated. "I got it, Jim!" she said unnecessarily. "I got it!"

I'd been dreading this all evening and was ready with my reply. "Never mind, Cynthia, it'll soon wear off." It was hurtful, I know, but in fact she never even heard me. Or if she did the words just bounced off. With a sudden laugh she did a little twirl there on the carpet, then turned and floated out of the room.

When at last she came down to earth a few days later I learned that at the close of the meeting George had invited all who wished to receive the baptism of the Spirit to go forward for prayer. Cynthia had almost leapt out of her chair and had been one of the first to the front of the church. There, two or three Christians had laid hands on her and prayed over her, some in 'tongues' - those strange babbling sounds the Pentecostals called a prayer language - and before she knew what had happened she felt power flowing through her whole body, along with an overwhelming joy. Moments later she too was speaking in tongues.

I was not pleased. George's persistence, with Cynthia at least, had paid off and she had now experienced the phenomenon I had been fighting to save her from. The chances were he would now step up his pressure on me and so I would need a new line of defence. It was the one I'd been saving for just such an eventuality. "Of course I don't doubt that something's happened to Cynthia," I told George the following Friday, "but that doesn't mean to say it's of the Lord. The devil can counterfeit the works of God, you know. And as for this speaking in tongues lark, that's just a lot of mumbo-jumbo. It's all of the devil, the lot of it."

Evidently George had heard that argument before. Unruffled, he smiled and said, "Well, let's wait and see." At first I wondered what he had meant, but as the days and weeks passed by I began to understand. Cynthia was changing, but in no way that I could attribute to the enemy. She seemed to be getting so much more out of her Bible reading each day. She was spending far longer in prayer every morning and thoroughly enjoying it. She was more joyful in herself and more loving toward other people (including me!). And she seemed to have so much more faith to exercise each day in matters both large and small. That didn't sound like the work of the devil to me. In fact it sounded very much like the type of Christian life I had been exhorting people to live in numerous sermons down the years. And, ironically, I now realised I hadn't been living that kind of power-packed life, either.

But wait a minute, what was I saying? The thought had come so fast I'd been unable to check myself. Power-packed? Was that really how I had summed up Cynthia's new lifestyle? I hated to admit it, but yes, there was a new dynamic in her life. And then, to my annoyance, I remembered that verse from the book of Acts: 'Ye shall receive power.' That was the promise George had made so much of over the months. And now I saw that promise fulfilled in my own wife. It was maddening. I wanted so much to be able to dismiss this baptism business as heresy or at the least a bubble that would soon burst – but my years of experience as a Christian wouldn't let me.

When I allowed myself to be totally honest I had to admit that Cynthia had been blessed, and tremendously at that. Regardless of my own opinion of how she had come into this blessing, the truth was that she was going on with God. But worse than that for me was the equal truth that I was being left behind. This was what hurt the most. This was what left me smarting. And this was what began to eat away at me as I tried to get to sleep at night. I would lie there, tossing and turning and thinking how unfair it was. Why should she get blessed? Look at her lying there, sleeping like a baby. Even in her sleep she's getting blessed. It's all wrong. At the same time I had no intention of following her into that blessing. George could coax and push and even pray all he wanted – he wouldn't find me chasing after his Pentecostal experiences.

As the months dragged by it seemed to me this was my best line of defence. Denominationalism. I knew I couldn't prove a case against the baptism from Scripture (I'd tried that one but every anti argument had gaping holes in it), and it was no use trying to dismiss it as a now-you-see-it-now-you-don't illusion. Cynthia's deepening experience of Christ knocked that one for six. No, I would have to take my stand on the time-tested argument of tradition. I was a good Wesleyan. Why, I was now Superintendent of the Sunday school (with 100% attendance from the village children, no less). I was a respected Methodist lay preacher. Youth leader. Church steward. Circuit steward. A member of half a dozen Methodist committees. In fact I'd been a Methodist longer than I'd been a Christian. It was inconceivable that I should change now, and a good Methodist would never embrace the doctrines of another denomination. That was it, I would stand on the rock of my Methodism. A sound rock it was too, for it had given me everything I'd ever needed. My Bible, a belief in prayer, and ultimately an introduction to Jesus Christ Himself.

But then a strange thing happened. One afternoon I was out in the yard tinkering with a misbehaving tractor and thinking through my argument for the nth time when I remembered the question that had come to me all those years ago – the question that had brought the challenge to my heart: Do you really know me? Yes, thank God, I could truly say that I now knew the Lord well. Jesus was real to me. The Father was a friend. But there was a niggle at the back of my mind. What about the Spirit? Did I know the Holy Ghost? I twitched at the thought and tried to wriggle out of it.

Of course I knew the Spirit. It was the Spirit that made God real to me in my own experience. Without the Spirit there would be no communication with the Father, no awareness of Jesus. It was God's link between Himself and His people; the supernatural presence of God in the world. It was what the Father had sent into the world after Jesus had ascended into heaven. But the thought persisted. Do you really know me? The truth came to me as clearly as if a light had been switched on in a darkened room. Did I know Him? I'd always thought of the Spirit as an 'it'. A force, a power, a presence. Never a person – a 'he'. I put down my tools and wiped my hands on a grease-rag, leaning back against the tractor wheel. All these years and I'd missed such a lovely truth. The Holy Spirit was a person! Different from the Father, without a body like Jesus, but just as much a person. Of course! There was that phrase I'd often used from the pulpit: 'the Holy Spirit, the third person of the Trinity.' He was just as much God, just as much one who possessed all the attributes of a person. True, His work was to reveal Jesus, but that made Him no less a person in His own right.

The thought intrigued me – and at the same time disturbed me. For I could not escape the fact that now closed in on me. I did not know Him, Who was He, this mysterious and wonderful Third Person? What was He like? How could I get acquainted with Him? It's odd, but as I began to think of the Holy Spirit in these fresh, new, personal terms I no longer felt afraid of Him. I could feel my defences slipping away, at first with much apprehension but then with more and more relief. And I felt a great weight breaking free of my shoulders. The phrase, 'baptism in the Spirit', still left me cold and uncomfortable but the person Himself...

Over the next few days I searched for Him in the Scriptures, and a whole new adventure began to open up for me. There He was, right at the beginning of my Bible, in the first few words of Genesis. Present at the very creation of the universe: 'And the Spirit of God moved upon the face of the waters...' Throughout the Old Testament He was there, brooding over Israel's history and occasionally stepping into events, coming and going like the wind, just as Jesus had described Him.

On into the New Testament, bearing the holy seed to Mary, sealing the Saviour's identity with the visible manifestation of a dove, leading Jesus into and out of the wilderness temptations, clearly present throughout His years of ministry and His final great triumph on the cross, in the wings at the resurrection and ascension, coming in great power upon the first Christians at Pentecost, moving upon the Early Church and distributing His many supernatural gifts to individual believers.

And all this time I'd not known Him. Worse, I'd resisted knowing Him. I saw this clearly now. It wasn't just George and Cynthia I'd been fighting – it was the Lord Himself. What a fool I'd been. And what pathetic arguments I'd put up against Him. My Methodism didn't seem to count for a great deal now. And, to my surprise, nor did it matter.

By the summer of 1967 I was half-way there. "All right, Lord," I said, "I'm willing to be baptised in your Spirit, but I don't want to go babbling about in other tongues." I had a hangup about the gift of tongues. I knew from George that it was often regarded as the first outward sign that someone had been filled with the Holy Spirit, but I didn't want that happening to me. It was one thing to lay aside my Methodism, but quite another to be considered Pentecostal. Yes, I still had my pride.

But God graciously dealt with this last remaining reservation in a wonderful way. Had I sat down to think about what would help me over this final hurdle I would have said that I should like to talk to a man of God outside my own set of circumstances; a man I already had a high regard for; a man who knew his Bible and who had thought through these issues; and a man who shared my Methodism.

The person God sent along was all of these things. It was Dr Skevington Wood, The Lord's choice, of course, was perfect. As a

Bible teacher Dr Wood's ministry had been appreciated at conferences all over the world, and he was also a man I was pleased to call my friend. He came to us one Sunday afternoon in September, 1967, travelling down by train from his home in Sunderland to take our Harvest Festival service. Over tea we began talking about the work of the Holy Spirit, but our time was short and we'd barely got into the subject when we had to leave for the meeting.

With so many questions yet unasked I decided to offer Dr Wood a lift home in the car that evening (a round trip of 110 miles) and to hope for some answers on the way. We set off at about 9:00pm and in the course of the journey I opened up my heart, sharing with my friend the events of the past year, my personal battle, my discoveries, and of course my remaining reservations. "I want to believe," I said. "I want to be filled with the Spirit, and have whatever the Lord's got for me. But... well, I'm just not sure about some of it, like this tongues business."

His answer took me by surprise. Dr Wood, I learned, had recently returned from a ministry tour of the Far East where he had witnessed churches in revival, moving 'in the Spirit.' Their meetings, he told me, sometimes lasted all day, beginning as early as 5:00 am and developing from one hour to the next under a powerful anointing, right through until evening. People were being saved, healed, filled with the Spirit and delivered from demons. "It was like the Acts of the Apostles all over again," he said, "And, yes, there was speaking in tongues. Interpretations. Prophecies. Words of Knowledge. All the gifts. Gifts and miracles happening all the time. The power of God demonstrated through His people. It was incredible. Incredible but wonderfully real."

Then he turned to me. "Yes, it's of the Lord, Jim. And he can do it right here. Here in England, in Yorkshire, in Sandhutton. Seek the Lord, brother. Seek the Lord. Be open to Him. Let Him give you everything it pleases Him to give you, and then ask for more!"

I arrived back at The Limes just after 3:00am, tired but excited. Dr Wood's answer had been the spur I'd needed. There were no doubts now. No reservations. No conditions. "All right, Lord – your will, your way." I wanted whatever He would give me and I couldn't get it soon enough.

It happened a couple of mornings later. I was alone in the house and down on my knees before the Lord when it seemed as though somewhere far above me a dam suddenly burst and a great torrent of love poured down upon me, washing over me in waves until I was floating in the most wonderful sense of the Lord's presence. No wonder they called it the baptism in the Spirit! Yet somehow that now seemed too clinical, too limited, for as the wonderful waves swirled around me I found myself laughing and rejoicing, as uninhibited as a little child frolicking in the sea. It was refreshing, invigorating, and deeply, deeply satisfying, as though I had been lifted into heaven itself and was experiencing all the peace and love and joy that are the very heart of the Father.

"Thank you, Lord! Praise you, Jesus! Glory to God!" I struggled in my spirit for the right words, adequate words, and realised I possessed none. How limited was my natural vocabulary! Yet even as I was thinking this my tongue began to move around unfamiliar sounds; words I had never learned nor understood. I knew what was happening. I was 'speaking in tongues' - the 'tongues' of which I'd been so wary. But it wasn't the mumbo-jumbo I had once feared it to be; it was a proper language with syntax, expression, inflection. A language that emanated from the Spirit Himself and that reached way beyond the limits of my intellect to enable me to worship God on a new and deeper level. It wasn't a language that was forced upon me – I'd been so afraid of 'babbling' in a tongue that was beyond my control – but a form of expression which was mine to use at will. Clearly I could decide when to start speaking in this tongue and when to stop, how fast or slow to speak, how loud or soft to talk.

All this plus the sure knowledge that I had received a new and deeply satisfying form of communication with God. I don't know how long this initial encounter in the Spirit lasted. Five minutes? An hour? But of one thing I was sure when finally I got to my feet that September morning: this was the most wonderful thing to happen to me in 20 years of Christian experience. Why had I resisted so long? But I knew the answer to that. Neither George nor Cynthia had ever been able fully to explain the tremendous blessing that was to be enjoyed through the baptism in the Spirit, and even if they had I wouldn't have believed them.

Cynthia, of course, was ecstatic. It had been six months since she'd been filled with the Spirit and throughout that time my stubbornness had sustained an unhappy friction in the home. Now that was all over. But best of all, we were one in a new dimension of the Spirit. The relationship with George was healed, too. Every resentment was gone, every irritation forgotten. In their place was a deep thankfulness that the man had not given up on me. For the best part of a year he had refused to take 'no' for an answer and his perseverance had finally paid off. But what had made him so determined, I wondered, when for month after month I'd snubbed him or laughed him off?

"It was the Lord, of course," he explained through that familiar grin the following Friday. "Once He'd told me He needed you to be filled with the Spirit I knew I had to tell you and to keep on telling you. It was just a matter of staying true to the vision." I was intrigued.

"What do you mean, that he needed me to be filled with the Spirit?"

He laughed out loud. "Well, you don't think He's blessed you just for your own benefit? No, Jim, I believe the Lord is going to do a mighty work through you and Cynthia, and He's going to do it right here on your farm. You wait and see."

Things began to move that very evening. It was nothing dramatic, but pervading our meeting was a new sense of expectancy, a new excitement. And no wonder, now that the host had received his inheritance! Naturally I couldn't help but share with everyone what had happened to me, and seeing as I was the one who'd been preventing the group from moving forward there was now no stopping us.

From that point on we never looked back. Friday evenings now had a new purpose, a new power, and for the first time the Holy Spirit had real liberty to move upon us. It was beautiful just to watch people getting blessed.

In the midst of all this, God's hand was on the farming at the Limes too although sometimes it was difficult to see what he was doing. One of the darkest moments for any farmer is when he has to destroy his herd and that moment heart-wrenchingly came to the Limes twice, the first in 1962.

At that point everything was swinging along nicely. The books were balancing, our debts were gradually being paid off, we had 400 pigs and there was a little money left over for further speculation. But then one morning I caught sight of something that was going to take the spring out of my step. It was a morning when Dad happened to have dropped into The Limes. "Come and have a look at these pigs," I called to him. "Something's not right - they're not eating properly."

Dad scratched his head then threw me a troubled glance. "Better isolate 'em for a while," he said. "Time'll tell." They were no better the following morning and positively sick the next.

"It's swine fever, all right," said the vet, confirming our fears. "D'you know the procedure?"

I nodded glumly. We sealed off the farm and waited for the man with the gun from the ministry.

The man from the Ministry of Agriculture came down the same day and gave the pigs the death sentence - all 400 of them. Before he left he gave me an official notice to replace my hand-painted one: SWINE FEVER. KEEP OUT. THIS FARM IS UNDER QUARANTINE.

The next morning I hired an excavator and we dug a huge hole behind the barn. Then the men from the Ministry came out to destroy the condemned stock. Farmers have to be philosophical about such things, of course, but it was hard to be objective, standing there watching the marksman shoot one pig after another and then having to drag the blood-spattered carcasses out of the pens, across the yard and into the hole. This was my livelihood I was burying. When the killing was all done the straw was raked out and burned, then the men in protective suits moved in with their pressure- hoses and washed the place out with powerful disinfectants. It was all over in less than two hours. Adjusting to it was going to take a bit longer.

In fact the tragedy of the situation didn't even sink in until the following morning when in the grey light of the dawn I went down to the piggery and stood looking around at the empty pens with the sickly stench of the disinfectant in my throat. But it was the silence, the stillness which got to me the most. It was so unnatural. Almost uncanny. And then I realised what that awful stillness was. It was death. I suppose a number of quite natural questions might have presented themselves to me at that moment. How were we going to recover from such a setback? Could I make up the losses on the grain yields? Would the bank extend my loan? Should we take on more pigs? Had we been wrong in dealing in them in the first place? Why had God allowed it to happen?

But, strangely, none of these thoughts even crossed my mind. Somehow, instinctively, I knew that the Lord was still in control and that in His own way He would see us out of trouble. Which left the way clear for the one thought that did break into my mind - a thought which surely originated outside of myself. "This is like hell," it was saying. This terrible sense of cutting off, of separation is what awaits everyone who dies outside of Christ. This desolation will be the lot of every unbeliever. It was a hard way to be spurred on to preach the ever-lasting life of the Gospel, but it was also a reminder I was not likely to forget.

That same year, as though to balance the setback of the pigs, we received a tremendous boost on the land. As usual we had planted a potato crop and were now preparing to harvest. A surveyor from the Potato Marketing Board, to whom we were selling the crop, had visited us earlier in the season to measure up and tell us how many tons of potatoes we could expect. His figure was 45 tons. Out of that he reckoned we would have three tons of 'brock' - tiny potatoes that would be riddled out during the packing process - and so our total expected sale would be 42 tons. I was happy with that because I had extra bills to pay that month and the money would go a long way towards meeting them. So it was with some satisfaction that we began packing the potatoes the following Monday. The Board had asked us to bag up ten tons per day, which was a reasonable output for three men working together, and so we brought up the sorting machine to the potato heap and set to. By late afternoon every trace of the morning's smile had been wiped away. We had bagged up ten tons of ware and it looked as though we'd got a good third of the pile. Despondent, I sent up a silent prayer. "Oh Lord, there's not going to be 42 tons of potatoes here. There's not even going to be 30!"

I don't know whether the men had realised this but they certainly took notice the following day when, strangely, the situation was reversed. "I dunno," said one, as we completed another ten tons, "this pile don't seem to be gettin' any smaller." Which was true because we hadn't moved the sorter any further into the potato heap all day. And we didn't move it for the rest of the day, either. In fact that machine stayed where it was throughout Tuesday and Wednesday. By the end of that third day, having now bagged 30 tons, we were all amazed.

All, that is, except the man from the Potato Marketing Board. He was just puzzled. He'd come down to see how we were getting on and decided there was definitely something very odd going on. This man was dealing with potato mountains all the time and he knew his business. "You're not bringing in potatoes from somewhere else, are you?" he asked. He'd now taken delivery of 30 tons of potatoes and we hadn't yet got half the pile.

"Certainly not," I said, "We've only got the one heap." The following day he was back with his chief to measure the field again and when they came into the barn they were both shaking their heads. "It's not possible," said the surveyor. "You're sure you're not bringing in potatoes from somewhere else?" By now I couldn't resist a smile. "I'm sure, and the men here will bear me out."

He shook his head again and glanced at the potato heap. "Doesn't make sense," he muttered. "You're getting more potatoes out of the heap than it's possible to get." There was no answer to that. All we could do was carry on bagging. When at last we'd finished we had a staggering 62 tons of good- sized, saleable potatoes... and a story that was going to raise eyebrows for a good while to come.

Jim's migraines had continued ever since he'd gone over the handlebars of his bicycle as a youngster. God's supernatural power was to intervene in a quiet way there too. For a while, Jim and a few locals had a nice little money spinner going at the auction mart in Northallerton: shill-bidding on livestock to drive the prices up and then splitting the profits with the seller. Jim was also making a tidy sum from dealing in cattle himself but keeping track of the prices of the different cattle that he was buying and selling and the dishonesty of the shill-bidding was only making the migraines worse.

In spite of Jim's protests, God's word to him was uncompromising: "Get rid of everything that does not honour me. Your cattle-dealing is offensive to me. It's devious, Jim. It has to go!" Jim reluctantly counted himself out of the phony bidding. "'Ee, y'must be mad," they said. "Thee's taking this religion stuff too far, Jim. Giving up all that extra money? Yer'll be sorry, lad, wait and see!" The cattle dealing business soon went the same way.

Yet somehow the farm continued to prosper. They had more money in hand than they had ever had and the migraines that had been especially bad following a hectic afternoon of cattle trading disappeared entirely. It wasn't that they gradually became less intense as Jim grew more relaxed; the Lord healed him once again. One week the migraines were there, the next they were not.

There was one more lesson to learn before Jim and Cynthia were ready to make the move to Hollybush and that lesson came the second time swine fever reared its ugly head. It was all sickeningly familiar: the sign on the gate, the hole in the ground, the crack of the marksman's rifle, the powerful disinfectant sprays. This time a full one thousand pigs had to be destroyed.

"Well, it doesn't alter the fact that God loves us," said Cynthia, matter-of-factly. "But, yes, maybe we'd begun to think that if we walked in the Spirit nothing could touch us." I thought about it for a moment, then nodded.

"I suppose you're right. Naïve, weren't we? How many times have we read Scriptures warning us to expect trials and tribulation?"

"The fiery trials," Cynthia muttered absently, engrossed in a delicate piece of needlework. We fell silent and I sat guiding Joanna through her favourite picture-book while I thought about that phrase.

A few days later I came across some startlingly apt verses in the Old Testament, in the book of Habakkuk. "Although the fig tree shall not blossom, neither shall fruit be in the vines; the labour of the olive shall fail, and the fields shall yield no meat; the flock shall be cut off from the fold, and there shall be no herd in the stalls: Yet I will rejoice in the Lord, I will joy in the God of my salvation."[5]

It was remarkable. This almost forgotten book of the Bible was speaking right into our situation. *Though there be no herd in the stalls.* That was us, all right. *Yet I will rejoice in the Lord.* Could we do that? Could we still say, "Lord, we love and trust you," when the mainstay of our income had just been wiped out?

There was no doubt in my mind that this was what the Lord was saying to us - that He wanted us to be able to praise Him at all times and in all circumstances. Not only when things were going well or when His hand of blessing was evident in our lives, but when the bills were mounting up and the pigs were being killed off outside our back door.

Not that we could ever praise him because of those circumstances, but certainly we needed to learn to praise Him in spite of them.

Once again it was through the presence of George Breckon in our lives that things began to change. In mid-January of 1968 George stamped the snow from his boots in our hall and asked: "Are you thinking of buying more land, Jim?"

"Whatever gave you that idea? We've only just got straightened out after that pigs business. In fact I've only just finished paying off the loans we've had these past ten years. There's no way I'm taking on more land, not for a good while yet.

He sat with his back to the range while Cynthia brewed a pot of tea.

"What makes you ask?" I enquired.

---

5   Habakkuk 3:17-18 (KJV)

He smiled uncertainly. "Well, I had this vision, see - a vision of you, Jim, looking out over a vast area of land."

I chuckled to myself. I'd had 'visions' myself that had turned out to be my own imaginings. "Sorry, George, but I think you've got the wrong man. If God wants to increase me He'll have to make two blades of grass grow where now there's one. Cake?"

Later, when he'd left, and I was over in the barn putting out the feed for the cattle, I had a chuckle over George's suggestion. Buy more land, indeed! Not when I'd just got myself straight. And then I put it out of my mind.

It was two months later, in early March, when the subject came up again. Cynthia and I were driving up to Northallerton for a meeting early one evening. It was only a short drive of eight miles or so and I knew the road so well I could have driven into town blindfold. We knew every feature of the landscape, too; every paddock, every copse, every gateway, every farm. Over there was Mr Scaling's place - a compact holding of 120 or so acres. And there, that was Eric Bell's land, with the rising hill and woods forming the boundary. Just ahead, around the bend, was a place that was up for auction: Hollybush Farm. It was quite a farm, 200 acres divided by the road with a big, imposing house. Someone with the right sort of money would have a handsome property in Hollybush Farm. I wondered how much it would go for; the auction was next week. In a million years, I wouldn't have guessed who was going to buy it. As we sped by the gateway with its sale board swinging in a bitter March wind I suddenly knew. "I want that place for my glory." It was that voice again, clear as a peal of bells on a frosty night. I swallowed hard. Oh, Lord! Where was I going to get that sort of money?

The Lord wonderfully confirmed his word on our journey home that evening, and this time the revelation was Cynthia's; something caught her eye as we passed the entrance. "The glory,

Jim I saw the glory!" It could have been nothing else; there were no street lamps, in all the years we had driven past the farm we'd never seen an outside light shining and the farmhouse stood a good 60 feet from the road. As we talked I felt all apprehension slipping away.

There was a silent impression in my spirit to go and see Eric Bell, the owner of the farm across the way from Hollybush. To me, Eric Bell was Pharaoh: a rich and successful farmer, and I was just a chicken! Next morning I rose to find encouraging confirmation in my Daily Bread Bible reading notes with the story of the rich farmer. Five minutes later, as the car crunched up the driveway into Leachfield Farm, I saw Mr Bell crossing the yard, a new-born lamb under each arm. He stopped and waited for me to leave the car, and as I got out I remembered Moses again – how he'd told the Lord he wasn't up to speaking to Pharaoh because of a speech impediment. I knew how he felt.

"G-good morning, Mr Bell." He offered his hand as best he could with the lamb tucked under his arm, and gave me a quizzical look. I looked him in the eye and said, "God sent me." I don't think anyone had ever said that to him before. Having almost dropped the lambs, he now clutched them with such a grip that I thought any minute they'd need a healing. "It's about Hollybush, across the way. Are you interested in buying it?" He nodded.

"As a matter of fact, I am – but not all of it. Why? Are you interested?"

I smiled. "Aye. But, like you, only in part. The Lord's told me I'm to buy the house and the ninety acres on that side of the road, and you' re to buy the acreage on this side here, adjoining your own land."

He shook his head. "I'm afraid that isn't possible. I've already made an arrangement with my neighbour along the road, Mr Scaling." My heart sank. I'd been so sure. "I can't go into details," he went on, "but Mr Scaling's going to have the house plus a few acres, and I'm having the rest."

"Oh, I see." Where did I go wrong? "Well, sorry to have troubled you." Dejected and confused, I drove back home and shared the bleak news with Cynthia.

"I must have misheard the Lord," I told her. Or had I heard Him at all? I went out to work with my head spinning. "What's going on, Lord? Did I get it all wrong?"

When I returned to the house at lunchtime there was a message. Cynthia couldn't hide her excitement. "Eric Bell telephoned. He wants to meet you at one o'clock." Back I went, my heart racing. It must have been a simple misunderstanding.

"I've had a word with Mr Scaling," Eric Bell told me, "and he says if someone else is interested, he's really not bothered about the house. He was only going to speculate with it, anyway. And the bit of land he wants is on the boundary, where his farm meets mine. I can let him have that, all right." I nodded.

"And my proposal?"

"I've been thinking about that – in fact it would suit me very well. Come on inside and we can talk." We agreed that each of us would come up with a price for our own half of the property and that the total would be the maximum we would go to in the auction. But as I drove back to The Limes I swallowed hard. I had just committed myself to a substantial business deal – talking big figures as if they were pennies not pounds – and yet I didn't own much more than the shirt on my back. It just had to be the Lord, or I was in trouble.

"And, just as a matter of interest, Lord," I said out loud as I turned the car into The Limes, "how much am I supposed to pay?"

The answer came back with alarming swiftness. "£34,000." I swallowed again. In 1968 that was a small fortune. Later that afternoon, with Cynthia and Joanna in the back seat, we drove up to Hollybush to see what we were buying. But not for a minute did we view the place with the critical eye of ordinary home-buyers. This was to be the Lord's house, and if He'd chosen us to live here we knew beyond a doubt we'd be happy. What better than to dwell in a house that God Himself had singled out. And so as we were shown around by Mrs Sowerby we barely took anything in.

The one impression we did receive was the size of the place. What would we do with 15 rooms? So few people in such a big house! Evidently it was something Mrs Sowerby was aware of. "If you buy this place," she said, "it needs to be filled with people." Her words could almost have been prophecy.

Before we left I had a walk out over the land to test the soil, just as Dad and I had done down at The Limes. But this time I was assessing the land merely out of interest. There was no decision to be made, no wondering whether this soil was a good investment, for the decision and the investment were the Lord's. Even as I came back across the fields to where Cynthia was waiting in the car with Joanna, I seemed to hear that silent voice within. "You just be here, Jim, and I'll prosper you."

This was Friday and the auction was the following Wednesday. That evening, at the Friday fellowship meeting, we shared with the group what the Lord had revealed to us and what we'd done about it so far. This caused quite an excited stir among our regulars. "Yes," they agreed, "this is of the Lord."

"But we need to pray about the money," I reminded them. "Right now we don't have a bean to bid with. I hope to see the bank manager on Monday morning, but it may be the Lord has other plans."

The bank was to be only part of the provision. On Saturday morning I had a telephone call from our good friend Ernest Hutchinson. "We've been praying about what you were sharing last night, Jim, and the Lord has spoken a clear word to us. 'Lend what thou hast to thy brother.' We've £8,000 invested. It's yours to borrow for as long as you need."

After I'd put the phone down I made a call of my own. I'd woken that morning with a name in my head. Kit Calvert. I knew Mr Calvert well, of course, from our long and mutual association with the Wensleydale Evangelistic Crusade, but I somehow knew that on this occasion his name had come to mind not in connection with outreach but because of his wide experience as a businessman.

An hour later I was sitting in Mr Calvert's lounge up at Hawes sharing with him the vision of a new work of God at Hollybush Farm, and asking him about borrowing money from one of the agricultural mortgage companies. He was not impressed with the idea. "I'd steer well clear of that sort of involvement," he told me. "Stick to your bank and whatever you can borrow from your friends." Before I left Mr Calvert had proved his own friendship with a loan of £6,000.

Monday morning found me sitting opposite my bank manager in Thirsk, outlining the Hollybush project and explaining that I had only £14,000 and needed a loan of £20,000.

"I expect you'll be wanting a little more than twenty thousand, with legal fees and so on. I'll get the paperwork drawn up today." I walked out into the biting March winds, mentally reeling at how easy it had all been. But of course it had. When would I realise that when God is at work His children just sail through. But borrowing money is relatively easy. It's paying it back that's the problem!

Back home I told Cynthia that the first year's interest on the loan would be around £3,500. "And then we've our own tax to pay, our tithes and offerings to give, our living expenses – and only then can we start paying back the actual capital."

She set a mug of tea down beside me. "Well, the Lord'll provide. He's never failed us yet. Look at George – sold up his farm, gave most of his money away, and been living by faith from that day on."

"Hey, that's a thought," I cut in. "I'd forgotten all about George's vision!"

I dialled his number up at Northallerton, "George, it's Jim. Do you still have that vision of me looking out over land? If I took you to a certain place do you think you'd be able to tell me if it fits what you saw? Do you know Hollybush Farm?"

I met George at the gateway just after three in the afternoon. Before we went in I quickly told him all that had happened in the past few days and then I called at the house to ask Mrs Sowerby if I could show a friend round outside.

"That's it! That's exactly the vision. Glory to God!"

The morning of the auction arrived and there was much excitement in the house. It hardly seemed possible that within a few hours we'd be clinching the deal that would bring Hollybush into our possession. We'd had word that there would be other interested parties making a bid for the farm, including a brewery that wanted the house for one of its directors and an entertainments company that had designs on turning the property into a sophisticated night-club, but none of these worried me. God had said He wanted Hollybush for His glory, and He was going to have it.

Even so, a telephone call around noon came close to hitting the panic button. "It's Mr Scaling," Cynthia called to me from the back door.

"I want to meet you outside the hotel, half an hour before the auction. Is that all right?

At 2:15pm I dropped Cynthia off at Mr and Mrs Hutchinson's home in Northallerton – the three of them to pray while I bid – and I drove on to the Golden Lion Hotel. All the way there the worry about Mr Scaling was snapping at my mind like a terrier at my heels. The previous day I'd had most of my teeth out and now had a thick scarf wrapped around my face to keep out the bitter cold. With that and my cap pulled down against the wind I looked more like a gangster than a businessman-farmer.

But how wrong I was. Mr Scaling, I discovered, had been sent by the Lord. No, he wasn't interested in Hollybush, but he did want to see that Eric Bell and I got the place. He was older than both of us, more experienced in sales-room techniques, and determined to steer the auction of Hollybush Farm to a satisfactory conclusion. In short, he was there to father us, and for that I was so thankful. If Dad had still been alive he would have been here with me today, but as that wasn't possible the Lord had sent along Mr Scaling with all the fatherly advice we could use. Confidently, he ushered us into the inner sanctuary of the hotel ballroom – suitably transformed for the occasion – and marched us down toward the front. "Buyers always sit in the second row," he directed. "Jim, you sit there, then me, then Eric, and Nigel on the end." Nigel was Mr Bell's son who presumably had come along for the fun.

Obediently, we did as we were told. Mr Scaling turned to me and said, "Jim, you' re bidding. But don't start till I tell you." My scarf was hanging round my neck now and I gave my mentor a toothless grin. It was 3:15pm before they got round to Hollybush. Together we listened to the auctioneer's glowing description of the house and land – the place God wanted for His glory – and then the bidding began. Forty thousand. Forty-five. Fifty. Fifty-five thousand. Shouldn't I be bidding? But the look on Mr Scaling's face told me he knew exactly what he was doing. Sixty thousand. Sixty-one thousand. A nudge in the ribs – and my hand shot up. Sixty-two thousand. From over there – sixty-three. Me – sixty-four. Up went the bids, a thousand at a time, until I was bidding on the edge of my seat. Seventy thousand. Seventy-one. I swallowed hard. The joint limit I'd agreed with Mr Bell was £72,000.

"Sold! Over here for seventy-two thousand pounds." That was at 3:21pm. At exactly the same moment, in the front room of the Hutchinsons' home not a quarter of a mile away, Cynthia was leaping to her feet, rejoicing as a conviction suddenly sprang up within her spirit. "He's bought it!" she cried. "I saw the hammer go down and I heard Jim's name! He's bought it!"

Hollybush was the Lord's. We had access to the house from the beginning of May but we chose not to move in until we were ready: floors had to be scrubbed, walls washed and papered, woodwork painted... While we were at it we decided to have the old fireplaces removed from the bedrooms. It seemed sensible to get all this done before we settled in, but we'd never realised what a job we'd taken on.

But for the willing help of so many good friends, plus the expert assistance of Cynthia's builder brother, Tony Biker, with the fireplaces, we would have been slogging away till Christmas. Even so, the house wasn't ready until late November. We couldn't wait to get all this finished, of course, but perhaps even the waiting period was in the Lord's plan. Perhaps he was teaching us patience.

A prophecy was given in our lounge at The Limes one evening. Brian Smithyrman was the Lord's mouthpiece that night. **"And it shall be, saith the Lord, that this place shall be called a place of miracles – Miracle Valley – for here will I perform great and wondrous things, the likes of which you have never seen before A place of miracles it shall be for even as the sick and suffering come and step upon its holy ground** they shall receive healing from the Lord. Yes, this place shall be known as Miracle Valley - a place where the Lord God of heaven and earth abides, and where His glory shines for all to see."

Miracle Valley! What a prospect! What a promise! And what rejoicing that word from the Lord caused that evening. We were more impatient than ever to get into Hollybush. We didn't wait to dedicate the place to the Lord. In fact, we did so on the very first Friday that the property became ours. About 20 rejoicing Christians met with us at Hollybush that night, and together we marched around the outside of the house, singing praises and confirming the territory as the Lord's. Then we moved inside, claiming each room for God as we passed through the house, and finally ending with a session of prayer and praise in the kitchen.

We prayed again in that kitchen, just Cynthia and myself, the evening of the day we finally brought our furniture in. Cynthia sat with three-year-old Joanna on her knee while I perched on one of the many tea-chests, committing our new home to the Lord, commending our little family to His keeping, and thanking Him for all the good things we could look forward to here at Hollybush. I could barely wait for next Friday!

The solid old house was almost vibrating with expectancy that first fellowship night. As the people arrived and we ushered them through the kitchen and up the stairs we saw excitement on almost every face. What wonders would the Lord perform in our midst this night? The way into God's miracle-working presence that first evening was as it had always been, through the doorway of thanksgiving and praise. No one in our group of 30-odd needed coaxing to rejoice in the Lord's goodness and we sang ourselves hoarse.

But as we settled to prayer we found our thankfulness gradually giving way to a much deeper emotion - our unworthiness. And as the Holy Spirit moved upon us we realised afresh something of the holiness of the God we loved. Tears were quick to flow, and before we knew it a sobbing brokenness had totally transformed the spirit of our gathering. We had cried together before, of course, but this was something new, and something that was to characterise many of the meetings in coming weeks. It was as though God was laying a foundation for the work He had planned for Hollybush, and that foundation was to be bedded in the tears of a broken spirit and contrite heart.

But if weeping was necessary before God would manifest Himself, then weep we would. It was worth every tear when, all at once, we became aware that the Spirit was among us. And when George stood up to teach us from the Word (we'd asked him to come and pastor the Friday meetings) it was as though the Lord Himself was speaking, such was the anointing of God in the room.

When it came to sharing personal needs no one hesitated. God was there with us and we each one knew that if we asked for His touch He would not pass us by. Besides, He Himself had called this place Miracle Valley...

"I'd like prayer for my knee," said Mrs Hutchinson. "It's been playing me up no end this week." She reminded us that years ago she'd fallen and broken her knee-cap and had suffered discomfort ever since. The pain had worsened recently because of the many hours she had spent scrubbing floors here in Hollybush House.

"Right, let's gather round sister Hutchinson," George directed, but we needed no encouragement to pray with this dear lady; even before we laid hands on her and asked the Lord to touch her knee we knew she would be healed. What we didn't expect was the bonus healing that was to come with it. For some years Mrs Hutchinson had been deaf in her left ear – so deaf in fact that even in the dead of night, if she was lying on her right side, she couldn't hear the ticking of the alarm clock. But that night God had breathed healing into her whole body and she couldn't get to sleep. After an hour of tossing and turning she nudged her husband. "It's no good, Ern, I can't get a wink of sleep with that clock ticking away." And then she realised – God had healed her hearing, too. Mr Hutchinson put the clock outside the room and then they went to sleep, rejoicing together.

Even after the move to Hollybush, the Wilkinsons were still heavily involved in the Methodist church at Sandhutton: Cynthia played the organ for the morning service, Jim was a lay preacher around the circuit and they were both committed to the Sunday school. But just like a lot of other folks at Hollybush, the church where they were involved wasn't too keen on the idea of the Holy Spirit. In fact, I've heard a similar story at least another half dozen times: people were baptised in the Holy Spirit and their church leadership were so intimidated by the obvious power and authority that they were asked to leave.

It came as a shock when a member of the church drew us aside after the service one morning and asked if we could give him a few tips about running the Sunday school. "I understand you won't be with us much longer," he said.

I stared at him. "Oh, is that right?"

"Well, I thought you knew. They've asked me to take over when you leave." It had been coming for a long time. I suppose it had begun after we'd been baptised in the Spirit, though it wasn't the baptism itself that had sparked things off because we'd been careful not to say too much about it in the church circle. But certainly the new zeal and boldness we'd received as a result of the baptism had stirred things up. As we motored home we could think of only two reasons why they should be planning to get rid of us: jealousy and fear. Jealousy because they had watched us throw ourselves into the children's work and had seen the way we had got results: 100% village attendance, with some youngsters committing their lives to Christ. And fear because the bogeyman that had haunted them ever since we'd joined the church had finally got the better of them: they were simply afraid that Jim and Cynthia would take over.

And we had taught the kids the gospel and that had meant repercussions in the home. One Harvest we taught them about keeping the Sabbath holy. When we came out of the church we saw combine harvesters and trailers driving past. I'll never forget those kids' faces as they stood and watched members of the church riding by on their way to work. They just couldn't fathom it. One minute we'd been teaching them how important it is for Christians to keep the Lord's day, and the next they were watching a group of men - church members - doing the opposite to what the Bible said.

There was no doubt about it, our total commitment to God and His day had been a thorn in the side of our fellow church members, and with complaints from non-churchgoing parents to back them up they had finally decided it was time to get rid of us.

The crunch was to come the following month at the annual church leaders' meeting, and in the intervening weeks I became more and more uncomfortable about any sort of showdown. It seemed the only thing for it was to resign. This was a corner we were being forced into, and it was almost unbearable to think that we would be leaving the children in the hands of a man who, as far as we knew, wasn't even a committed Christian. But there was nothing for it but to commit the situation to God and bow out gracefully.

Even so it was with swirling bewilderment that we entered that downstairs room at the church that November night. The prayers of our friends back at Hollybush were with us, we knew, but nothing could remove the awfulness of walking into a room full of people whose hearts were set against us. In fact seeing the room packed was confirmation of what was going to happen. For the past nine years, the most we'd ever had at a church leaders' meeting was six; on those occasions nobody had been much bothered to take an interest in the work. But tonight was different. Tonight there were 25 people present - just about everybody who had a vote in the church's affairs. It was like walking into a courtroom where judge and jury had already decided that the accused was guilty.

When the future of the Sunday school came up on the agenda I didn't waste a second. "Mr Chairman, ladies and gentlemen, Cynthia and I have something to say before you go any further. Knowing the feelings of the church towards us, and unable to continue in our present roles in such unhappy circumstances, I regret that we have no choice but to tender our resignation from the Sunday school. In fact we shall be leaving the church altogether."

It had been the shortest and most difficult speech I had ever made, and as we drove back home we shared a wrenching of the heart, almost as though there'd been a death in the family. But we couldn't put the matter behind us yet. Having accepted our resignation the committee had asked if we would stay on until the end of the year to give the new Sunday school superintendent time to settle in. We'd said yes. In our hearts, though, we knew that our work for the Lord at Sandhutton had already come to an end. Even our resignation had been a formality. The end for us had come when the unthinking church member had let slip the church's plans.

We went up to bed that night with great sadness of heart. It was, we knew, the end of an era. The sense of loss did not hit us, though, until that first Sunday in January, 1970, when for the first time in our lives we rose on the Lord's day with no church to go to. It was a desolate feeling, a sense of being abandoned, of being out in the cold. "What now, Lord?" we cried. "You gave us the call to preach your Word and the Methodist church gave us the opportunity. What now?"

By this time the Sunday school had started at Hollybush, the various classes each occupying one of our six bedrooms, and so we knew we wouldn't be idle. But it wasn't the same. The children's work at Sandhutton, along with the Sunday night preaching engagements on the Methodist circuit, represented a lifetime's investment. We had loved the work and the people too. Could we let it go just like that? It was our first real valley experience. We could not even lift our eyes to see the potential of the Lord's work at Hollybush. After all, our Friday meetings, barn rallies and prayer meetings were just informal happenings - they weren't a church.

But therein lay the key to the future, as we learned one evening when the Lord spoke directly to us through prophecy. "Men have closed doors and I have closed doors, says the Lord, but as doors have been shut into one church I will make a way for you to go into every church. And as I have brought you out of one denomination I want you to be willing to participate with every denomination and to be friends with them. But do not affiliate yourselves to any one group, for I the Lord have brought you out of denominationalism."

So the Lord had been in it all the time. But of course! Why hadn't we seen it before? He wanted us to be free - free of traditions, free of the structures that hinder the working of the Spirit, free to do and go and be what He wanted, and no ties. It would take a bit of getting used to, of course, but if that's what God wanted that's what He would have. Above all, we desired to be in the centre of His will. It soon became clear that from then on we were to throw all our energies into building up the work of God at Hollybush, and when we began to do that our eyes were opened to the full potential of an independent fellowship that was totally available to God.

As we thought on this we realised how good it was to be free. No rules and regulations save the Scriptures. No historical ties bar the Lord Himself. No one to tell us what we should be thinking and doing except the Holy Spirit. Perhaps it was because I'd been so engrossed in the work at Sandhutton that I'd failed to appreciate just how much the Spirit had already brought into being.

Now, for the first time, I saw a unity and ongoing purpose behind the various meetings that had been started, realising that the prayer meeting, Sunday school and Sunday evening gathering had not come into being simply because they'd seemed a good idea or met a need, but because they had been ordained of God. Now there was another meeting, too. Since the Sunday school had begun, those parents who had travelled long distances to bring their children to the house had either sat about in the kitchen or waited outside in their cars. Now someone had suggested the obvious: 'How about a little Bible study and prayer time while we're waiting?' That was okay by us, and so yet another meeting began in the big room upstairs.

At last I had caught the vision. These meetings that had started as a spin-off from the Friday fellowships were not just 'added extras' but an integral part of the work God was doing. Each had its role to play and each complemented the others. Looking at it in this light it was exciting to see how the work had grown, and thrilling to contemplate the future.

That was at the start of 1970 and it was just a few weeks later when Jim and Cynthia came suddenly to their next valley experience. George Breckon was such an important figure in the early days at Hollybush. In George, the fellowship had a gifted and anointed preacher and teacher. So Easter 1970 came as a shock when George announced that he was to go as pastor to Valley Road Baptist Church in Northallerton (now New Life Baptist Church). For Jim, this felt like turning his back on the fellowship. Every story has two sides and George did not feel that the story as told in Miracle Valley fully reflected actual events. What was certainly true was that when George went to pastor Valley Road, he took dozens of Hollybush people with him. In fact, the Friday evening after George's announcement saw only six people sat in the big room ready to meet with God that night. These were difficult times for the people at Hollybush – the story in Miracle Valley reflected what the people, Jim and Cynthia included felt keenly as hopelessness and failure.

"What's going on, Lord?" Jim cried. "Where are all the people? If they're down at Valley Road instead of here, then why?" Some of the folks could not even pray that night; such was the gloom and rejection that enveloped them. Cynthia put their feelings into words: "Well, what now? Is that it? Is it all over? Is Miracle Valley finished?" Hollybush had been decimated – from about seventy regular attenders to about twenty.

Margaret Brown offered some wisdom on what went on at that time: "I absolutely loved George Breckon – one of the most amazing men I have ever met. He was just a totally committed, dedicated man of God. I love Jim too and for us it was tragic when the parting of the ways came but I'm sure you understand: as my husband used to say, 'You cannot have two leaders. It's a monster. Monsters have two heads.' And both these men were leaders in different ways. The parting of the ways just had to come."

"I think there was ten or twelve of us left. And I remember we were meeting in the upstairs bedroom and Jim said, 'We just have to call it a day.' I said, 'You can't do that. It's a miracle how God gave you this place and how he called you. He hasn't said He's finished with you. We're not giving this up.' Of course we didn't and wonderful things happened."

Of course, time heals all wounds. In the 90s, as families and young people were looking for something to get involved in, Hollybush folks were getting older and its youth group was dwindling. By then, George had been promoted to glory and his son Rodney was pastoring New Life with an active youth and families work. Rodney has now moved on and pastors Grange Road Baptist Church in Darlington.

George's wife, Gladys, was still involved at New Life, right up until her death just a few years ago. A slip of a woman, her hearing aid would often whistle all the way through her son's preaching - turned up to full volume so that she didn't miss a word. Rodney often joked how she had once burned out the clutch of her brand new car in just seven thousand miles. But even into her eighties, Gladys was a woman full of missionary fervour, only too happy to relate her and George's exploits in ministry, including as missionaries in East Africa.

Jim now speaks fondly of the Breckon family as friends.

Not surprisingly, many [families] found a new spiritual home at the New Life Church in Northallerton, where our friend Rodney Breckon was pastor. Rodney has strong links with Hollybush, having spent much of his time here as a lad. His dad, George, was of course a key figure in the development of this fellowship, and in my own growth in the Lord. Now George has been promoted to Glory, but he is remembered with a great deal of affection and it is gratifying for us to know that his son is leading a thriving church just down the road. We are glad, too, that strong links with the Breckon family continue through our fellowship with Rodney. As for many of our young people attending there... well, if Rodney's church was able to offer them what was not available at Hollybush at that time, we were not about to complain. As long as the youngsters were growing in the Lord, what did it matter where they were being fed?

BRANCHES

There are a few names that come back again and again in the stories of Hollybush Farm: Arthur, Edwin, Ernest, Irene... Maybe a great way to describe it is that the Lord is the trunk, Jim and Cynthia are the thickest branches but these four are some of the heaviest branches. All four of them are still a part of the furniture at Hollybush.

There's a good chance that Arthur Bennison's booming voice and infectious laugh will be the first thing you hear when you arrive on the farm. He and Jim will probably be tinkering with a tractor somewhere, or deciding on the best time to bring in the hay.

Arthur started coming to the Friday night prayer meetings while they were still at the Limes and had struggled with his back for years - injured while lifting milk-churns. God healed his back at a Sunday school anniversary service in Exelby but Arthur wasn't unaccustomed to God performing miracles. Always with a smile on his face, you're never quite sure if Arthur is joking or not. He had often quipped that, being in a constant state of financial embarrassment, it was always a miracle that he ever had the petrol to drive the 50-odd miles to and from the fellowship each week.

"It were no joke," he told Jim one day. "I was working for my dad up at Bilsdale and he wasn't able to pay any wages, only a bit of pocket money now and then. Rarely did I have any cash to put petrol in the van. It was a real dilemma for me and my equally penniless pal, John Mattison, who worked on a neighbouring farm. But we were determined to get to the meetings and so we told the Lord about it. That was when he sent the rabbits."

When Jim heard this, he thought he was in for some of Arthur's famous leg-pulling, but apparently he'd never been more serious. "Rabbits were fetching five shillings a pair, and in 1968 five shillings' worth of petrol would take you a long way. We first saw them on our way home from the meeting one Friday night. They were sitting there in the road, waiting for us, picked out in the beam of the headlights. If they started to move off all I had to do was flash the lights on and off a few times and they'd freeze right where they were, sitting up on their hind legs, their heads at just the right level to take a clout from the front axle. It was quick and it was clean - the butcher didn't want them if the skin was broken - and one night we bagged seven. Almost every week we got one or two - always enough for our petrol the following week."

When his father retired, Arthur hoped that, like his father and grandfather before him, he would be able to take on the farm but the landlord wasn't so keen. "What will you do for cash?" Jim asked him.

"Well, I suppose I could catch rabbits," he said, grinning. "John and I have got that down to a fine art."

"Or you could come and pick potatoes for us here at Hollybush," Jim ventured. "We could use an extra pair of hands."

And that's how Arthur came to Hollybush to work – he drove down from Bilsdale three or four days a week to help with the potato crop. It wasn't long before Jim was offering Arthur a job –

the lease on the Bennison farm had run out and Arthur had been seeking the Lord as to his future. God has shown Arthur in quite a dramatic way that he was to get behind the ministry at Hollybush.

"I wouldn't say it were a vision," he explained, "but I got this picture of Moses being supported by Aaron and Hur during the Israelites' battle with the Amalekites." The story is a well known one; a tough battle fought in the valley of Rephidim while Moses looked on from the hillside. God told Moses that his people would prevail so long as he kept his arms raised to heaven. When he lowered his arms the battle would swing in favour of the enemy. In order to achieve victory, Aaron and Hur had to help by supporting Moses' arms. "I believe that's the job God's got for me," Arthur said to Jim. "To support you in the battle."

Jim couldn't argue with that. "When can you start?"

Arthur started work the following week. There was sugar-beet and spring barley to sow, potatoes to plant, fertiliser to spread on the grazing pastures ... plus the numerous other little jobs that had to be done at that time of year. His experience and capacity for hard work were a real God-send.

But Arthur wasn't just a farm hand. He also heard from God on a regular basis. "I saw this sort of roundabout," he told Jim, "with roads going out from it like the spokes of a wheel. The roundabout, or hub, was Hollybush, and the roads led to other fellowships."

Two years earlier, Jim had first received another prophecy at the Limes: "...From this place, saith the Lord, there shall be a coming in and a going forth, for it shall be as a wheel within a wheel, the blessing which I shall pour upon you flowing out from your own circle to a wider circle beyond. This shall be the Lord's work, reaching far and wide to touch the lives of countless men and women, and bringing glory through it all to His name."

At the time, we were excited but had no idea as to how this reaching out to other areas would work. Now with Arthur's word, obviously it was time to act. The first step was to ask those who travelled so many miles to us each week whether they would like our help in starting a fellowship in their own area. The response from three directions was a very positive 'yes'. So began a very hectic phase of outreach from Hollybush that was to involve Arthur and me travelling many hundreds of miles almost every week for the next two or three years.

On Monday evenings we drove to Dolphinholme, near Lancaster, a round trip of 160 miles. Wednesday evenings saw us heading out to Hesketh Bank, Southport, a round trip of 184 miles. And on Thursdays we travelled the 110 mile round trip to Silksworth in Sunderland.

This ministry always happened after a full day's work on the farm and it was often gone 2:00am when we pulled back into the yard. Yet another miracle was that Jim and Arthur always woke with the dawn, totally refreshed. In fact the day never dawned when they rose yawning and sluggish, if the previous night they'd been out on the King's business.

The vision of Hollybush Camp was first revealed to Arthur too. "Hey, Jim, the Lord's just shown me, we're going to be having a camp meeting out in that field beyond the barns." Jim wasn't convinced but Arthur was adamant that this was a God-given revelation. Privately, Jim thought the prospect of having a camp meeting at Hollybush highly unlikely. Besides, with two farms and everything else going on, there was enough to organise without getting involved in another big project. And tent meetings, Jim knew, took an awful lot of organising.

But it wasn't long before God confirmed this vision and not long after that, the marquee was booked, the lighting and PA systems

arranged, chairs organized, toilet facilities on order... and to pay for it all an account had been opened at the bank under the name of Hollybush Christian Fellowship - the first time the name had ever been used officially.

Arthur told me a story which serves as an excellent introduction to Ernest Allison, a man with a perpetual twinkle in his eyes. I think it's probably because he's fully aware of the radical faith that he has lived out over his 77 years and how implausible his stories really are. In fact if they weren't told to me over a cuppa in the café at Hollybush, I probably wouldn't believe them myself but in this place, you come to expect the unexpected.

Here's the story that Arthur told me: "We were smuggling Bibles behind the Iron Curtain – Ernest and I went a time or two. I think '72 or '73 because my wife and I got married in '74 so we fell in love while smuggling Bibles! We started in Yugoslavia, and then we went through into Hungary."

"There was a little lass called Mary Feldy who had been smuggled out of Yugoslavia and was supposed to go back in a fortnight but something happened that she couldn't go so she stayed with us there in the big house [at Hollybush Farm] and learned the language. After that, every time anybody went from here they went to pick her up as translator."

"When we went through the border from Yugoslavia into Hungary, she walked through alone. We waited a bit until she got through and out of sight a bit and then we went through, stopped and picked her up and went on our way."

"We had one address in our head, not written down: on the Miskolc Road out towards Russia from Budapest. And off we went – that's all we had in our heads. We had nothing written because if anybody found it we'd be in trouble."

"Well, we took the sides off vans and packed Bibles in all the gaps: took the interior off the side of the van and then stacked them all in and put it back on. There must have been at least a hundred Bibles. We took clothing and other things but we didn't tell them that it wasn't ours - we left it all. The van was full of stuff – engine oil for the pastor... We came home a lot lighter!"

"We had trouble in one or two places. We had a prophecy given in Yugoslavia that we'd go through a very dark place, feeling as if somebody is watching you. We went out the Miskolc Road from Budapest and lo and behold, we had to go right through the middle of an army camp. The prophet didn't know we were going that way but they gave us the word. One of the boys said, "What do we do?""

"'Well,' I said, 'prophecy was given to keep going – don't stop. Keep going forwards.' Anyhow we went through and the Lord protected us all the way through. Beautiful, it really was."

"We set off home on the Friday night and we landed back into Thirsk on the Saturday night when they were having a meeting in Austin Reed's, the clothing factory. I think they had just got started in the meeting when we landed in."

Andrew van der Bijl (known as Brother Andrew) was one of the first to raise awareness of the plight of Christians behind the Iron Curtain and went further by smuggling Bibles to those in Communist Eastern Europe. His first trip was in 1948 and was the

inspiration for many other Christians and organisations to get involved. Some of the stories that smugglers tell are of God's amazing provision and intervention. Arthur's story seemed so unbelievable until I spoke to Ernest who took the whole thing to a whole new level...

"In '71 they had a meeting of the church in South Otterington. They wanted volunteers to go out and take Bibles. And I volunteered, the same year my boss died and left a legacy. So what he left we used to go to Yugoslavia. It was only a hundred pounds. The whole family – my wife and five children. With five small children, they thought we were just on our holidays. The guards just waved us through! We were in a car with the tent on top. Sleeping bags and everything; under everything were Bibles. We didn't have a single problem except one time I thought I'd gone the wrong way and had to turn back and then another where I was driving on the wrong side of the road!"

"Another time I went, we went through Hungary into Romania and we got caught and put in detention. The European cup was on and they were more interested in that than they were in us so they just left us to sleep in the armchairs in the waiting room. They said they would have to take us to town. All they wanted to know was the names addresses of the people we were delivering them to. We were daft as brushes. We put on our thickest Yorkshire accents and said we didn't know the addresses. They couldn't even understand what we were saying half the time because of our broad Yorkshire accents. There was a great big well-built officer in charge who said, "You won't go anywhere – we've got your passports and we've got people with guns.""

"When we had left here, we didn't know that the prophecy was that we'd go through fire and we'd come back joyful. They searched the car and took some of the Bibles out but they didn't find all of them. So the ones that we had left, we went back into Yugoslavia and delivered them to Mary's cousin."

Ernest grew up in a place called Thornton Watlass – just two and a half miles up the road from Snape. Thornton Watlass is a tiny little hamlet; fifty houses and a few farms in the hinterland. Smaller even than Snape and not big enough to support its own chapel, Ernest and his family went to church in Snape and that's how he knew Jim. Ernest and his brother used to go to Snape for the Guild rallies and for three or four years were under Jim as Guild secretary. When Jim moved on, Ernest had two or three years doing the same job.

As a talented musician, Ernest was pressed into the Guild groups that ministered around the countryside, often being called upon to accompany Cynthia's singing.

"In those days, we used to go from one church to another – if there was a Guild rally or a church anniversary or a Harvest Festival, we used to go along to the different churches and support them. Especially since there was always a good feed involved!"

"I had been working as the head gardener for a Sir who lived in some fancy hall. So when Jim got this place, he asked me to do the garden before he even moved in. So I was here a bit before anybody else!"

"We used to come on a Friday night up to the big house and bring our whole family. We would put all the kids in Jim & Cynthia's bed and then go into the meeting. Five kids! And then when there were barn rallies in the granary, the kids would come wi' us and sleep under the chairs while we were worshipping and jumping and praying and shouting. It didn't seem to disturb them."

What Ernest doesn't mention is that all five of those children who used to sleep in Jim and Cynthia's bed during the meeting are all

still now born again, filled with
the Spirit and going on with
the Lord.

As always, God's timing is perfect – just after Ernest had been
made redundant from his previous job, Jim was ready to employ a
driver and farm hand and Ernest has been a fixture ever since.

Edwin Gill is a wise and gentle man who has worked for Jim on
and off for 35 years, first working the farm at the Limes, then at
Hollybush too and like Ernest as a driver for Jim's haulage
business. To spend time with Edwin is to spend time with a man
wonderfully at peace with his lot in life. He is content to walk and
work on the land. He has no need to travel and see the world.
Above all, he is immensely happy – something that he told me at
least a dozen times when I interviewed him. And it comes across
in everything he does and says.

"I grew up in a little Methodist chapel over in Nidderdale. It's
actually the chapel I got thrown out of, because I got filled with
the Holy Ghost. Dad was a local preacher all my life. Mother was
one of the most loveliest, gentlest women I've ever met. There was
me, my sister and my brother, Kenneth who became a bishop in
India and then in Newcastle."

"I can remember getting saved as if it were yesterday. When the
altar call was given, I just felt that nudge of the Holy Spirit. I
didn't know it was the Holy Spirit then. But I knew I had to get to
the front and I ran to the front and bawled my eyes out. It was
Easter 1948, just before my eleventh birthday. I can still see it in
my mind's eye.

The first time Edwin met Jim was in 1957, about three months
before Jim and Cynthia married. Edwin was living in Nidderdale
and going along to a youth club at a little Methodist church. Jim

came to preach and Cynthia came to sing. At the time, Edwin was going out with a girl and that was the night she got saved.

Edwin had made his plan when he left school: he wanted to be a farm manager. So he had worked through various farming jobs and eventually moved to Killinghall near Harrogate. He went there as cowman but within two months, was running the farm, lock, stock and barrel: 60 acres and 35 cows which he had doubled to 70 cows by the time he left, five years later. As far as anyone was concerned, he had made it; he was living his dream.

"1976 was the year that everything changed in my life. God just challenged me," says Edwin. "We were travelling to Hollybush meetings, doing over 200 miles a week from Killinghall. We used to come on a Friday night as a family. We'd maybe go up the Dales from here on a Saturday. On Sunday I had to milk my cows, get my breakfast, all the way over here for the service, back home, lunch, milk my cows, tea, back again for half past six. That was Sunday. And then the prayer meeting on Tuesday night. Wednesday night was the youth group so one or the other of my wife or I would come."

"God spoke to me he said, 'You've made it now. Will you let me take over?'"

"That year we came to Hollybush camp and my whole family were baptised in the river. As I came up out of the water I was slain in the spirit. That's when I got filled with the Holy Ghost."

"In 1979, my wife had been at a prayer meeting without me. She came home and said, 'Jim's wanting a man to live at Sandhutton. Over the years I'd been working at The Limes and at Hollybush too. In fact I had cleaned a lot of bricks and did a lot of knocking of the buildings down on my days off. Jim told me the job was mine if I wanted it."

"I was milking the cows on the Wednesday afternoon before camp and I used to have the radio on. In those days, they used to broadcast evensong and that day read a scripture from Acts 16. I

noted it but thought no more about it. At the camp that night, somebody referred to it again. On the Thursday night camp meeting, I can't tell you who was preaching. I can't even tell you what he preached about but he read the self-same scripture: Acts 16. It said, 'Paul and Silas came out of prison and went to dwell in the house of one of God's servants.'[6] It just hit me like a ton of bricks. I went to Jim after the meeting and said, 'I'm coming Jim.'" And my remit from the Lord was just be here on the farm and in the fellowship. Whatever came my way, I did it. 35 years later I'm still doing it and still happy. I'm still living in the farmhouse at Sandhutton. As far as I'm concerned, I'm happy to carry on like this until I drop dead."

"To begin with, I was just doing whatever needed to be done but before long there were two wagons – Ernest drove one and I drove the other. I used to move a lot of hay and straw for a local straw merchant. When he had a heart attack and he packed the business up, Jim asked me to take it on on his behalf. "

"The haulage business was very successful for many years but in 1999, I said to Jim, 'I just feel in my spirit that this hay and straw job is going to dry up. I can't tell you why because I don't know why. Do you want me to look for another job?'" Jim disagreed – he had promised to keep Ernest and me until we retired and that was how it was going to be."

"Yet by the end of 2000, the straw business had indeed started to dry up. Jim ended up having to make both Ernest and I redundant but it wasn't such a problem – I was only eighteen months away from retirement anyway."

"It was just amazing how it all worked out, how God had it all planned out beforehand. After I was made redundant, I was turning work away, there was that much that was happening. I finished working with Jim in January 2001 and what should

6   Acts 16:40

happen in March? Foot and mouth. The hay and straw business would have gone down the pan anyway. Lorries and tractors couldn't move round the countryside without all kinds of paperwork. God was taking care of things in advance before foot and mouth hit. It had to be God for there was no other reason that a successful business would just dry up like that."

"I'm very happy just to be here. What I call just to be a servant. I don't need a title. I've been called farm manager and it made no difference. At Sandhutton I was one of the lads with Arthur here and myself. It's just like old times even now. Ernest is 77, same age as me. Arthur's a bit younger. Jim's 84... We still got hay in this year."

"People are always on about this, that and the other. I've often said to people, 'Just find out what God wants. It's as simple as that. Find out what God wants for your life and just get on with it. You know? Don't argue, just do it!' I've found even now - I've bad problems with my legs but God gives you the strength. If you're where he wants you, he'll not ask you to do more than what you can do. I was chatting with someone only last weekend and they were on about, 'I can't do this and I can't do that.' And I let them go on for a bit and I said, 'Whoa, that's enough! What can you do? If that's what you can do, do it to the best of your capability. Forget what you can't do. I can't do a lot of stuff now. I couldn't run down that field for anything. But I can walk down it.'"

"And when you find out what God wants, you just get on with it. It makes life so much easier. You don't have to worry about even whether you're going to wake up in the morning. You just go to bed and if God wakes you up you wake up. If you don't you're in a better place. In glory already."

"I'm involved with the prayer team a lot, at camp time particularly. I never miss a meeting, very rarely unless I'm away on holiday or whatever. I've had a bit of prophetic input over the years which has been part of my remit."

"I'm happy just to be here. Other people go to far off places but it never seems to have been something that has been on my agenda. I've been to America once. But still today, if I never went beyond fifty miles it wouldn't bother me."

"At camp, I'll be in the café at quarter to seven in the morning at the latest. I'm working there while ten or half past. Washing up, cutting carrots up, peeling potatoes. I'm happy. I don't want to do anything else really."

Edwin is a man circumspect about life's trials and his own advancing years. Perhaps he knows the story of a hymn that he quotes by Horatio Spafford.

This hymn was written after traumatic events in Spafford's life. The first was the 1871 Great Chicago Fire which ruined him financially (he had been a successful lawyer and had invested significantly in property in the area of Chicago which was decimated by the great fire). His business interests were further hit by the economic downturn of 1873 at which time he had planned to travel to Europe with his family on the S.S. Ville du Havre. In a late change of plan, he sent the family ahead while he was delayed on business concerning zoning problems following the Great Chicago Fire. While crossing the Atlantic, the ship sank rapidly after a collision with another vessel, the Loch Earn, and all four of Spafford's daughters died. His wife Anna survived and sent him the now famous telegram, "Saved alone." Shortly afterwards, as Spafford travelled to meet his grieving wife, he was inspired to write these words as his ship passed near where his daughters had died.[7]

When peace like a river, attendeth my way,

When sorrows like sea billows roll;

Whatever my lot, Thou hast taught me to know,

---

7   http://en.wikipedia.org/wiki/It_Is_Well_with_My_Soul

It is well, it is well, with my soul.

Refrain: It is well, (it is well),

           With my soul, (with my soul)

           It is well, it is well, with my soul.

Though Satan should buffet, though trials should come,

Let this blest assurance control,

That Christ has regarded my helpless estate,

And hath shed His own blood for my soul.

My sin, oh, the bliss of this glorious thought!

My sin, not in part but the whole,

Is nailed to the cross, and I bear it no more,

Praise the Lord, praise the Lord, O my soul!

For me, be it Christ, be it Christ hence to live:

If Jordan above me shall roll,

No pang shall be mine, for in death as in life,

Thou wilt whisper Thy peace to my soul.

But Lord, 'tis for Thee, for Thy coming we wait,

The sky, not the grave, is our goal;

Oh, trump of the angel! Oh, voice of the Lord!

Blessed hope, blessed rest of my soul.

And Lord, haste the day when my faith shall be sight,

The clouds be rolled back as a scroll;

The trump shall resound, and the Lord shall descend,

A song in the night, oh my soul!

"My wife who had been saved the first time we met Jim and Cynth had big problems with her eyes. 17 years she struggled, on and off. Once she'd been taken into James Cook Hospital in Middlesbrough. We'd been helping with a fellowship over at Marske at the time and I remember singing with them, 'Whatever my lot, Thou hast taught me to know, It is well with my soul.' When I went in to Middlesbrough in the afternoon to see my wife and she'd got her sight back in one eye but the other one never did come back. So she struggled with that for years and years. It must have been 17 years or so."

"It was on May 3rd, 2009 at camp in the Sunday morning meeting. I used to set my wife down because she couldn't see that well. All the ladies would come and so she had a good laugh. That morning was no different, just the same. We were going through the meeting and it came to the breaking of bread. She took the bread herself and took it and she said, 'I can't see, love.'"

"We'd been praying that the Lord would heal her. I said, 'Lord let this be the day.' But I wasn't ready for what happened. I took the cup and put it in her hand. She took it, give it me back and that was it – the last time I spoke to her. She had a stroke there and then and twenty six hours later she went home."

"I think that was wonderful, how we took the breaking of bread together and then she went. But this is one of the things that really blessed me and has blessed me and always will is that the person who sat on the other side of her was Cynthia who led her to the Lord. I said, 'Can somebody ring for an ambulance?' Somebody was on the phone for twenty minutes while the ambulance arrived and that person was Joanna. And the person that was the other side of the bed holding her hand when she actually went home was Jim."

Irene is a name and a woman shy of the limelight. Farming communities are incredibly male-dominated both in their make-up and their outlook. Hollybush is no exception – when you talk to Jim, his stories are all about Earnest, Edwin, Arthur and others. He doesn't talk so much about Irene but I dig a bit deeper and Joanna is the one to tell me that Irene was a big part of her own childhood and has been as much a part of the story of Hollybush story as anyone else. Yet her name only appears twice in Miracle Valley. Irene's contribution has largely been in the background – Joanna rolls her eyes a little when she says, "You know farming communities; they're not really into women and women in leadership... The women make tea!"

"Irene came to live with us when I was still quite a young age. And she helped a lot babysitting me. She's great; she's quite a character and she's forthright with her opinions! She used to work in a launderette when we were still at Sandhutton. She used to live at Sandhutton with her mum and she used to do some work for mum and babysit for me back then. So when they moved up here and her mother died, my parents took her in."

There are a few other names that come up again and again and again in the stories of Hollybush: George and Gladys Breckon, Tommy and Jean Spence, Ian and Margaret Brown, Terry and June Brown... People who have been around since almost the very start.

Tommy Spence, Margaret Brown and Terry and June are the only ones still with us – the rest have gone to glory.

Vintage Hollybush sign with the wrong phone number

Hollybush House

The Old Granary

Hollybush's New Hall, 1979

New Church Hall Opened In 1992

Hollybush Farm as seen from space!
Imagery © 2015 DigitalGlobe, Infoterra Ltd & Bluesky, Map data © 2015 Google

Youth Camp 2002

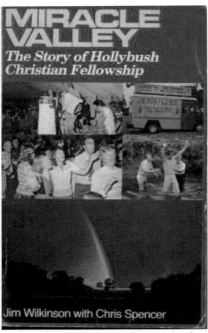

Book Cover from the original
Miracle Valley book

First Camp Water Supply

Early baptsims: 1974

Children's Meeting:
Praise & Worship

First baptism: August 1972

The great barn fire of 2005

Selwyn Hughes with Jim

Two young ladies from Altrincham

Arthur Bennison and Michael Neiland (now promoted to glory)

Evangelists Stewart & Chritine Dawling – faithful friends. (Christine wheelchair-bound for almost 20 years, still smiling!)

Feed my sheep

LEAVES

The leaves are the things that are there all the time. They're the things that you expect to find on a tree – each one individual and beautiful on its own but so numerous that we often forget they're there. Like wallpaper or the passing of the seasons, we don't give them much thought until they change in Autumn and are suddenly a thousand times more beautiful.

There are a few things that Hollybush has always been about which can easily be take for granted: preaching and teaching the word of God, evangelism discipleship and the work of the Holy Spirit. These things are like the leaves on the trees at Hollybush. Right back since his days as a Methodist lay preacher, Jim has been an itinerant preacher and evangelist. He doesn't ever miss an opportunity to encourage someone to know the Lord. In a conversation that any evangelist would be proud of, I once expressed my dislike for black pudding. Jim responded, "No you're right: I'd rather eat the meat off the pig. I don't go in for blood much." And then with a twinkle in his eye, he added, "Except for the blood of Jesus! Hallelujah!" To this day, Jim continues to travel and preach locally and around the country. He counts it a privilege to have been welcomed by every denomination to do as 2 Timothy 4:2 suggests: "Preach the word; be prepared in season and out of season; correct, rebuke and encourage—with great patience and careful instruction." Friday night prayer meetings, Sunday services, Sunday school classes, midweek fellowships, family and youth camps, local missions and all manner of other activities continue apace at Hollybush.

Even now, after all these years, a group of believers gather on Hollybush farm to worship, pray and receive what God has to offer every Friday evening. Of course, they aren't in the big old farmhouse any more, that's been sold on and Jim and Cynthia live in a much more manageable bungalow built a few years ago. The upstairs bedroom got too small for the prayer meeting so they moved out into the granary. When that got too small, they built the small church and when that too ran short of space, they built the big church. A 400-seater sanctuary will probably keep them going for a while! These days there's a sound system, a band and the words are projected onto a screen. They don't sing choruses out of a hymn book any more but they still wait with expectation for what the Holy Spirit is going to do.

Come 7:30pm, Jim will be standing at the pulpit welcoming people and inviting people into God's presence. They're sometimes part way through the second song when the drummer shows up. They were once part way through the third song when Jim showed up. "Well, you all made it before me tonight. Hallelujah!" he joked. And just like they've done on this farm and at The Limes before they moved, the believers will settle to prayer and worship. Like the leaves on a tree, each prayer meeting is individual and beautiful on its own but after almost half a century, they keep passing by, one week to another.

How did Friday nights get started? Simply because nobody else seemed to have a meeting on a Friday night. It started as a local preachers' prayer meeting for the Methodist circuit in our kitchen at Sandhutton. Some of the local preachers would meet together to pray. Of course, when George Breckon came along, people started to get filled with the Holy Spirit and things stepped up a gear. People like Arthur, John Mattison and others began to turn up. The local preachers by and large stopped coming as we began to get more Spirit filled. As the things of the Spirit started to manifest themselves, those who weren't necessarily wanting that began to tail off. All except one and his wife: Mr and Mrs Allinson, who lived in the same village as we did at Sandhutton. He was the village milkman. They took us under their wing when we got married, living just round the corner and they spurred us on in what we were doing.

Hollybush has a knack of punching well above its weight in the visiting preachers who take to the podium on a Friday night.

We get a lot of people we don't know. We don't really get anywhere to hear people. Usually it's a recommendation from someone we know. It doesn't matter what denomination they are as long as they love the Lord. And so we've always had a good spread of speakers. Lots of people have phoned up and said, 'Hey we're just coming to England,' or, 'We're just in England. Have you anybody for Friday night? Have you a night? We're passing by.' And that's how we get people from Australia and all over. Itinerant evangelists who are in England: people from the States and other places. David Carr, he's the boss of the Elim place and David Shearman, the Assemblies of God man. We've had people like Bob Gordon [evangelist & Bible teacher], we had Colin Urquhart [vicar & charismatic leader]... Some of these men were here before they got well known. Once they get well known, they get a choice of where to go and we might not see them again.

Then there's Bill Wilson [founder of Metro World Child, America's largest ministry to children] who comes comes once a year. He's a big name, he doesn't need to be coming to Hollybush to preach but there's one or two humble men still around and that's Bill. The first time I met bill was about 14 years ago. It was at a conference and Bill Wilson was one of the speakers. At 11 o'clock there was a cup of coffee or tea and everybody jumped off the platform. Bill picked up a plastic bag and in there was a couple of sandwiches. He said, 'I just like to keep sat here,' but he told us to come and chat. That's Bill Wilson. He doesn't nobble with anybody – he knows what he's doing; he's a guts man. He's where the rubber hits the road and there's not many people like that. He's not looking for high places. You love him or hate him. He comes once a year. I would get him for camp but August is one of their months when big things are happening – school holidays, 8,000 kids under canvas. God is really in that work. Janine is one of our people. She went to work with Bill Wilson and with their helpers they feed over 2,000 children once a day every day through Metro Ministries on the rubbish dumps in Nairobi.

Another of Hollybush's regular activities that passes year to year is Hollybush Camp – spoken of reverentially because it seems like all the best Hollybush stories revolve around camp.

It took Jim a while to come round to the idea of having a camp at Hollybush after Arthur first had a word from God. But when he moved forward with it, God gave Jim a word of his own: "An American evangelist will be taking meetings at the first camp. Well, on the day before the camp was due to begin, Jim took a phone call from a friend up in Scotland. "I understand you've a camp meeting starting tomorrow. Is that right? Can you use a speaker? Our man up here is redundant." Earlier in the week, a young woman had committed her life to Christ at one of their meetings and this had caused considerable trouble at home. Up until then she had been living with her boyfriend but knew she could no longer continue the relationship and told him that he would have to move out. Not taking too kindly to the idea, the boyfriend burned the tent down and they had to close the crusade. "We'll send this man down to you. His name is Wilbur Jackson. He's an American evangelist."

"He's the man we're waiting for. Send him down!" exclaimed Jim.

Later that night, after a great deal of rejoicing in the granary, an army of believers marched out on to the site where the marquee stood. They did a complete circuit of the field, singing praises all the way round and stopping in each corner to claim the field for the Lord and to post warrior angels to watch over the camp.

That first camp meeting saw 150 campers filing into the marquee for the first ever Hollybush Camp. And

God used that camp week to draw people to Himself. People rushed forward to the platform to give their lives to Christ.

More prophecy was fulfilled when a man who had been emotionally in a very bad place got saved and then brought his son back the next night who was saved too. This was after a prophecy that said, "I will send to the tent a man and his son and I shall save them."

Each evening, God's glory increased. More people were counselled than the night before and each day they heard more stories of how God was dealing with Christians in their quiet times in the privacy of their tents and caravans.

When the week finally ended, everyone was asking, "Will there be a camp next year?"

It was with a heavy heart that they packed away the chairs and dismantled the tent. If only the camp could have gone on, if only they could have lingered in that wonderful sense of the Lord's presence...

"Amazingly, those of us working the farm were able to do just that. Arthur was first to put it into words. 'Have you noticed that tremendous peace out there in the field where we had the marquee? As you walk across that patch of ground you can really feel it, as though the Lord's presence is still there, brooding over the place.'

"D'you know, Arthur," Jim said, "I reckon it's because of those warrior angels we posted in the four corners of that field. We never dismissed them. I reckon they're still out there on duty."

Arthur tells us a bit of the history of camps at Hollybush:

"In one sense, you see, there was no camps ever about in 1972 when we had our first camp. There was maybe one or two at the most but now there's camps all over the place. So the first two or three years, there was over a thousand camped. The first camp ever there was

150 camped at the other side there where the caravan park is. And then more people came in on an evening. And then the following year, we had two fields full and our neighbour had a field and a half full too. That was over a thousand camping and others dropping in. They were standing round church. The balconies were all full as well."

"That was in the early days, now there's camps all over. Nowadays there's three to four hundred people. That's day visitors as well as campers. There's a lot of people come in to the different guest houses in Thirsk and Northallerton. They'll ring up and ask where's the best bed and breakfasts to stay. It's just remarkable. Things have altered over the years. Possibly more so now because we're in the church rather than the tent. Folks used to see the tent and they could hear it too because of the sound. A lot of folks in the village here if it was a nice night would sit out and listen to the singing, you know. If you were talking about it, 'Oh yeah, we were sat in our garden listening.'"

"In those days we just had a piano and a book: the Cliff College Chorus Book. That's what it was in the early days – that's how it began. And then we had the Redemption Hymnbook and then the overhead projector. Of course now it's all computerised."

For those who were around before the advent of overhead projectors, the Redemption Hymnal was the first 'Pentecostal' hymn book; with it's famously bright red cover, it contained 800 evangelical hymns. Compiled by leaders from the three main Pentecostal denominations in the UK (AOG, Elim & Apostolic), it was and is strongly associated with the emergence of the Pentecostal movement. And much to Jim's delight, it included a liberal smattering of Charles Wesley's greats.

The preface proclaimed: "This collection of hymns has been compiled to meet the need of companies of believers all over the British Isles who are rejoicing in a scriptural experience of the grace and power of the Holy Spirit similar, they humbly affirm, to that received by the early Christians on the Day of Pentecost, and enjoyed throughout the primitive apostolic churches... A hymnal is now proffered that combines rich devotional hymns in abundance with stirring revival hymns that present the gospel in all its depth, winsomeness and simplicity."[8]

Camp numbers have gone up and done. From 150 in 1972, they got up to about 1,000 in the mid 90s. These days, the camp meetings still have about 3-400 faces, both new and old. Of course, Hollybush also has its annual youth camp and rents its field out every year to Urban Saints for their Spree weekend ('Spree is a camping weekend for young people (ages 8-15) and their leaders. At the heart of Spree are opportunities for young people to have riotous fun and discover what adventurous faith in Jesus looks like.'[9]) and to Kairos Christian Youth Camp ('Kairos is a Christian youth camp that exists to help young people engage with God, each other and to go home better equipped to live out their faith.'[10]).

But what's really interesting is the number of stories of God at work that have the word 'camp' in them. Bernard's foot is only one of a long list where God has chosen to work during the Hollybush Camp. It has an atmosphere that is a cross between a family reunion and a village fair. Camp is when the wider Hollybush family gets together. The folks who have moved elsewhere come back. In the mornings there's always a first rate Bible teacher. Last year it was John Andrews, part of the faculty at Mattersey Hall Bible College and long-time friend of Hollybush. Then of an afternoon they have a plunder round the Missions Mart and catch up with their friends over a whistling kettle on a gas camping stove in their caravan awning. Or they nip into Northallerton on an afternoon for a sneaky pot of tea and a cake in Betty's Tea Room. And then in the evening, they eat their

---

8   *Redemption Hymnal* (Music Edition),
Rickfords Hill Publishing, 2006, page v.
9   http://www.urbansaints.org/events/84
10   http://www.kairoscamp.org.uk/

dinner and come into the big church, more expectant than ever that God's Holy Spirit will descend in power.

Jim wonders aloud with a few stories when asked why so many of Hollybush's best stories talk about camp.

Why? Same as today: because God showed up and did things that we couldn't. People have come from all over. There was a group came from Germany and they said, 'You've got to be careful with that girl because she's demon possessed. You've got to keep your eye on her.' Anyway there was one night she just dropped on the floor and started writhing about like a snake and upsetting everybody. Anyway we just went across and prayed over her, told her to get up immediately because we'd prayed with her and the testimony was that God set her completely free that night. We got letters back from Germany telling us that she was absolutely free and was pressing on with the Lord. Two or three years later she came back for camp again.

We've seen a lot of what we would term deliverances or people being set free. There just seemed to be lots of that about, more so at camp than on Friday nights. There was chap came who was into pornography. It was the first person we came across like that but he was printing pornographic stuff at Harrogate at a printers. Anyway, God set him free as well and he's still free all these years later.

It's just a sovereign act of God. When people see people being changed, they start to hope and expect that God might do something for them too. There was a man came for two or three years. He had a three wheeler car, a Robin Reliant. And he came from somewhere near Hull because that's where the factory was. Anyway, one year he got healed completely just by the laying on of hands. He'd had an accident years before so he had those leg callipers. He was on the dole and disability benefits and he got miraculously healed but he didn't lose his benefits because they wouldn't believe him. He told them he wanted them to take the car back because he didn't need it and wasn't entitled to it. They told him they couldn't do it; he had it for life and though they could see him walking, the paperwork said he would need it for life so they couldn't take it back off him.

And August Ericson down in Lincoln. He was a fish and chip man. There was a night when something happened whether he tripped or whatever. Anyway he got his hand right up to his elbow in the fish fryer. On the Friday night, God told him to come up to the meeting and we prayed with him. He was all wrapped in jelly stuff but God healed him. He took his dressing off the next morning and he was completely healed. Four days after it happened he was back at work. So when people are there in the meeting and see these things happen, they begin to hope for things for themselves.

Then there was a chap from a little village called Kyo [it comes from how County Durham people pronounce 'cow'] up in County Durham. At the end of the meeting he came forward for prayer and they were having a job to hold him down. I was praying with some others but I said, 'What's happening lads? Eh, just get off him a bit. Come on, let's have a look - sit back.' He sat up on his backside and he had a caliper on because he had one foot about four inches shorter than the other. And he got it off and he flung it against the side of the tent behind the stage and it went down behind the stage. 'Thank you, thank God for that. Thank God. Thank God,' he shouted. His foot grew and he was healed. He lived in a row of seven dwellings, he and his wife. When he told the rest of the people in the street, everyone in that line all became Christians. We had the calliper hung in the barn for about six or eight years after that.

Missions Marts is one of the ministries that's been running at Hollybush for thirty years under the watchful eye of June Arrowsmith. Up until recently, it was run as its own separate charity – began in 1984 with the collection of clothes which were sent out to a children's home in Africa. From that small beginning emerged a work which involved the collection of clothes which were sent abroad and the selling of clothes, bric a brac, books, etc. and the money raised was sent primarily abroad.

"When I was a little girl, I was sent to Sunday School at Corporation Road Baptist Church in Darlington. There were quite a lot of folks from the baptist church who used to come here – maybe thirty of us. And one of the couples started having meetings in their home. But I was sort of put out of the church when I was baptised in the Spirit. They said we weren't allowed to have the meetings any more. They didn't want to know and they wouldn't let me pray with anybody. But God said to me, 'What I've put within you is part of my testimony.' So they said to me, 'You better find another church if you feel like that.' The minister said to me, 'You'll be back in six months, June.' That was thirty eight years ago. The first time we came, we went to a meeting in the granary and we thought we were in heaven; we just sat in worship for an hour and a half. It was the late seventies. It was absolutely fantastic."

"We started the Mission Mart over thirty years ago in 1982. Why did it start? The lady was in here yesterday; her husband was a missionary in Kenya. He came home on furlough and said, 'Is there any way you could get some children's clothes out?' He was working with and orphanage you see."

"I was a teacher in Darlington, so I put a notice up and asked the mothers if they would bring anything they had. So they brought things in and my friend used to help me pack them – we packed them into boxes a bit smaller than a banana box. It used to cost us about fifteen pounds each to send them, but we sent off as much as we could."

"Then the Kenyan government decided they didn't want their people wearing inferior clothes. They had to be made locally in Kenya. So I asked Jim, 'Can I sell some things at camp?'"

"It started with just one table. I just sold clothes at first but then it sort of got bigger. In those days I was still teaching. I've been retired for about seventeen years now. As soon as I retired it sort of mushroomed. People bring stuff in from all over. We don't know where all the stuff has come from. We just get boxes and we sort them out and price them and everything."

"We've had all sorts of people come in. The most unusual thing we've ever had given was a boat. They brought this boat into the barn with the mast up. I said, 'How much do I sell it for?' I didn't even know what it was worth! Fifty quid we got for it!'"

There's a notice board on the way into the big church that trumpets the Missions Marts achievements:

Money raised:

1984	£199	1995	£3,140	2006	£12,000
1985	£250	1996	£4,138	2007	£12,238
1986	£500	1997	£4,008	2008	£12,000
1987	£609	1998	£5,006	2009	£18,061
1988	£1,057	1999	£6,040	2010	£15,537
1989	£2,226	2000	£6,015	2011	£11,125
1990	£2,378	2001	£6,825	2012	£11,009
1991	£2,362	2002	£8,740	2013	£13,900
1992	£2,850	2003	£8,000	2014	£1,929
1993	£3,271	2004	£10,500		
1994	£4,529	2005	£9,980		

Total: **£200,422** Praise The Lord!

Some of the groups who have received gifts of money or goods are:

- John Green – Orphanage in Kenya
- Kays Farm Fellowship – for their children's homes in India, Nepal, Thailand & Myanmar
  - Philippine Outreach Centre
  - A. Staley – Children's work in Brazil

- Global Care
- P & Leslie Gomez – Philippines
- Eurovangelism – Poor & destitute in Russia
- Don Bell – Labourers Ministries International
- Chinese Church Support Ministries
- Bibles for China – Peter & June Gregory, Melvin Banks
- Phil & Vanlal Walters – Thailand
- CART – Containers to Africa
- Margaret & Derek Wheldon – Brazil & Africans
- Novi Most Relief – Russia
- Chance – Brazil
- Barnabas Fund for the Suffering Church
- House of Hope – Disabled children in Bethlehem
- Bishop James Kotey – Ghana

In late 2014, the Missions Marts trustees decided to wind up the charity. With an increasing workload and the advancing years of most of the volunteers, the opportunity was taken to do something different. With a newly emptied barn, there's some excitement about what might happen in that space. Joanna has some ideas about opening it up to the community and June is still more than willing to be involved, "Even if it's just serving teas and coffees!"

One of the things that Missions Marts has been faithful in helping has been the Bibles To China initiative, spearheaded by Peter and June Gregory. Peter is part of the leadership of Hollybush and also one of the trustees. Quite by coincidence, I get to hear his story as I'm sitting in the office with Jim. He comes in to borrow some keys and gets talking.

Peter is a retired Anglican clergyman, a story full of miracles in itself.

"I had eight parishes and was running round like the proverbial headless chicken. At 58 I was pensioned off; the doctor told me I was going to be dead before I was due to retire and they very quickly pensioned me off. We were coming here on a Friday night so after I retired, we came here full time. It was then that God opened up an amazing thing."

"When my wife and I were students at Durham University, we both felt a call to China. Of course we're talking about 1962 when I was in Durham so there was no way of going to China then. Chairman Mao was in power in those days and no Westerners came in our out."

"Our son eventually became a school teacher and he went to teach in a school in Hong Kong. That was in 1996 and he said we should come out for a holiday. I'd been retired two years then and my health had begun to pick up."

"So we went to Hong Kong for a holiday and while we were there, we were offered two alternatives. We didn't go looking for either of them but the Lord sent them anyway. The Dean of Hong Kong Cathedral said, 'Now your health has picked up, come and work with us – I'll give you a parish on one of the islands.'"

"But more exciting still was a Chinese guy we met who said, 'Come with me into China and I will introduce you to the underground church.' When we met them, they said, 'Why don't you come and teach us the Scriptures?'"

"Since then we've been twice a year for three months at a time into China to the underground church. I'm afraid now we've got a bit older, we've not been this year. It's the first time we've not been for 16 years. It was 37 ½ years from when we were called until when we put foot down in China."

One of the biggest ways that Hollybush has been able to get behind Peter and June's ministry has been in sending Bibles to China. While definite numbers of Chinese Christians are hard to come by, two independent surveys in 2007 counted about 40 million Protestants and about 14 million Catholics among China's population of

1.3 billion. Yet China is still high on the list of countries where Christians are persecuted for their faith.

For a long time, it was impossible to lay hands on a Bible in China – the Communist government had banned them and owning one was punished severely. Some organisations continue to smuggle Bibles into China but although smugglers often manage to evade arrest or are deported, they can leave greater problems behind them for the local believers. Many charities find they can work legally in China and that it's far more effective in the long run – they can build relationships with government officials and local believers.

In 1987, the Amity Foundation set up a factory in China sanctioned by the Chinese government and to date has published well over 125 million copies of the Bible in local languages. The Bibles have an official government stamp in them meaning the owner of the Bible has nothing to fear. Amity are still the only factory with government approval to print Bibles in China.

It costs about £1 to print and distribute a Bible. Over the past few years, Hollybush has managed to raise over £100,000 which means 100,000 copies (of those 125 million Amity Bibles) of God's word placed in the hands of local believers in China, thirsty for God's word.

A big chunk of that £100,000 has come from the handmade cards available in the main church. It seems like something so simple, greetings cards that people need all the time yet because of this simple work, so many thousands of believers have been given one of the greatest blessings of all: a copy of God's word in their own language.

Hollybush and the Missions Mart has not only been a blessing financially for the people it supports in Kenya but has also been instrumental in boxing up and shipping supplies to Uganda and Romania. Thousand of sack of clothes have been sent to Africa and Romania over the years: 150-

200 boxes of clothes and other goods are sent every year along with sewing machines, typewriters, knitting machines, etc.

Christian African Relief Trust (Yorkshire) is run by local volunteers based in Huddersfield, West Yorkshire. It relies entirely on voluntary contributions. It has no salaried staff in the UK or overseas. As often as funds allow, a forty foot container is packed full to overflowing ready for dispatch from their Huddersfield warehouse. Each container costs on average about £5800 to send. They have an on-site charity shop which helps to pay for running costs and contributes towards the sending of some containers.

Hollybush continues to be one of their collection centres for donations of blankets, clothing, bicycles, computers, medical, educational and vocational supplies along with dried and tinned foodstuffs, school stationery and other specialist items.

Under the banner of 'Northern Aid for Romania,' a very similar operation is under way for Romania. Kola, a lifelong friend of Hollybush is a Romanian with his own lorry who has driven back and forth across Europe over twenty times now from near Bucharest to Hollybush and back; a 3,600 mile round trip.

The partnership has developed and a few people from Hollybush have been to Romania to help with the work. Annette (whose husband Bernard was healed in the first couple of pages) went with Maude (who you'll meet in a few paragraphs) recently.

"An old lady here [Maude] said, 'Annette will you go to Romania with me?' At the time I felt sorry for her. I thought, 'How old is she? 82!' She's just got married to a toy boy! So I said yes I'd go just to keep her quiet really. And the months ticked by and it was still there and I booked the flights and I just thought, 'Do it.' Before we went I decided that if we were going to go to Romania we should do something more thought out than just going to see because they're poor and they've got no money and they're hungry. I wasn't going out there to take photographs – I was going out there to work. And we worked for 3 weeks non stop."

"I was thinking that money wasn't the right thing for them. We wanted to help them to support themselves more and feed themselves and that's exactly what I said to the church. I said that we wanted them to sponsor a chicken for five pounds each which would buy the chicken and raise them for the next few months with food. When they get a bit bigger they'll be laying eggs, they'll be hatched out to chickens and they've got a business then, haven't they?"

"On the barn door of the chicken hut, it's got a sign that says Hollybush Blessed Chickens. It's our farm gate that we sent – our barn door that was in the container. They call them 'pui' there. And all the neighbours and all the people in the shop came in and kissed the chickens. They love them to bits."

"Arthur was the main star. He dressed up as a chicken in church and Jim couldn't control him. I got a chicken outfit at Easter and no-one would put it on for me but in the end Arthur did. And I was up on the stage doing a talk with a slide-show and everything asking for money. And then in comes Arthur, jumping up and down. I was trying to talk and he was flapping and crowing and handing out chocolate. Everyone absolutely loved it. Jim couldn't control him. He was saying, 'Sit down Arthur! That's it now Arthur, just sit down where you are.' And Ernie was playing the trumpet and he's got a bald head and Arthur put chocolate on his head while he was playing the trumpet. We named the cockerel after Arthur!"

"There's a hundred chickens and forty turkeys. They cost £500 and we raised £600 in one day. We bought some chickens the first day, then we were going out to the gypsy camps and the orphanages. And I ended up spending all the money that I'd taken to look after myself. All my spending money – I had to phone home and say, 'Can you please give me some more money.'"

"We went into an orphanage called Butterflies. It's for people with learning difficulties from 18 onwards. They had no food; the cupboards were bare. All they had for lunch was a tray of curried potatoes and not a big tray. And it was to feed 17 people, not even to feed the staff. For breakfast they got one slice of bread with margarine on. That was it. And at tea time they got a slice of bread with marg and a piece of meat on. And on a Saturday morning they got one 500g box of corn flakes to feed all 17 and 2 pints of milk. Very very poor diet and no food. And they were all like walking skeletons. So I spent all my money buying food for them."

"What they would love more than anything is potatoes. And there's farmers putting potatoes into ditches to rot with people in Romania starving and other parts of the world. It doesn't seem right, does it?"

When you start to spend some time at Hollybush, there's a phrase that you'll start to hear a few times: "Oh, he/she is a real character." I've heard it from enough people's mouths on the farm to realise that there's something going on here that's worth some deeper thought.

You see, if you're looking for a church full of people who have their stuff together, who are emotionally, financially and spiritually stable, then Hollybush is the wrong place to look. Perhaps that's part of the problem in a lot of churches – people work so hard at trying to fit into the mould of what a 'good' Christian should be that they don't leave any room for the Holy Spirit to do something amazing. In most churches, you don't meet many 'characters.' At Hollybush, it seems like every other person you meet is a 'character,' Jim, Arthur and the rest of them included.

Perhaps part of the reason for Hollybush's reputation is that it seems to attract, amongst others, people whose lives are in a mess. People that social services would describe as having 'complex needs.' Although to

Jim, that sounds awfully familiar – Jesus spent his time with sinners. Not just people who disagreed with him on a theological issue or who went to a different church or denomination; actual sinners! Matthew 11:19 tells us that Jesus' detractors accused him: "Look, a glutton and a drunkard, a friend of tax collectors and sinners!" As He told the parable of the lost sheep, the tax collectors and sinners were all gathering around to hear him – to which the Pharisees and the teachers of the law muttered, "This man welcomes sinners and eats with them."

And who were those sinners? Perhaps they were prostitutes and thieves. More likely (since it was the Pharisees directing the accusation) it was the people who didn't have their lives together. The people who weren't in the middle class, didn't own their own house or know how to drive a car. The people who had experienced abuse, abandonment and hatred from those they loved and who continued to face the consequences in their family situations and in the decisions that we're sometimes forced to make. The people who didn't fit the mould of what a good little Christian looks like. Why does Hollybush seem to have so many characters? Because that's exactly who Jesus would have been spending his time with.

Like Tom. Tom is a great big bear of a man from Northern Ireland who found himself in a church, disillusioned with Alcoholics Anonymous because it got people off the drink but didn't go much further. He found an old leaflet tucked down behind a pew that was a year out of date for Hollybush Camp and so he hitch-hiked the couple of hundred miles to get here and has been to every camp ever since. He gets up early every morning to clear up all the rubbish on the site. By his own admission, he's doing his best to walk with the Lord. But he also admits that he comes with a whole lot of baggage.

And John who has a couple of Land Rovers that he's converted into ambulances that live in one of the barns. It's a never ending tussle for space between the

Land Rovers and the containers going out to Africa and Romania. If you let him, John will bend your ear for hours; the End Times is one of his favourite subjects and he is a man who loves a good conspiracy theory: the Illuminati, the Freemasons and the Bilderberg Group. John is an immensely clever man but faith-wise, I'm not sure what he believes quite fits in with what Hollybush believes. But I'll tell you one thing: he's still here and has been for a long time. Something about what God is doing here at Hollybush continues to attract him.

Time after time, I hear stories of people with a past. People who have been at their worst point in life and somehow found their way to Hollybush. For lots of them, they've seen big miracles happening in their lives – life changing healing and supernatural answers to prayer. Yet consequences don't disappear overnight with God. Many of us still live with the choices we made as younger men and women, even though we're back in the will of God. Joanna will be the very first to tell you that testimony.

But to a man (or woman), they will all tell you that when they came to Hollybush, something was different. God is doing something here that lots of people find quite difficult to describe. Like the leaves on the tree, what happens here isn't a single event or experience. It's in all the different miracles, both small and large. It's in every one of the prayers that have been offered here – for God to intervene, for the miraculous, for healing, for release or even just the groans for when people haven't known what to pray. Hollybush is about each and every leaf – each time God has done something in the lives of people, whether seen or unseen.

And those stories happen so often that half of them are forgotten. Jim only remembers to tell me when something else triggers his mind. "Simple Faith: they're some lads from your homeland, from Belfast. You'll enjoy them – come back for camp and you'll see them," enthuses Arthur. But before Arthur's finished, Jim cuts him off.

I'll tell you what, the first time they came was two years ago, a miracle happened right before their very eyes. A lassie had been there worshipping, about eighteen or twenty years old. Right at the edge of the platform, she dropped dead while they were singing. I said, 'Right folks, everybody get praying.'

Anyway we had medics on the job and two doctors were there in the congregation. Somehow, whether through prayer or whatever they got her going again. They said that if your heart stops for more than three minutes you're a goner and it was just short of three minutes. She sat up and because the ambulance had already come on its way, they took her to see if she was all right. There was no brain damage at all and when she stood up, I said, 'Right folks, let's thank the Lord; let's have a praise time now.' We've never had a prayer time and a praise time like that before or since up to this time.

I ask Jim if that's the kind of story we should put in the book? "You can do. Well, yes because everybody saw that. We just forget about these things!"

We had a woman phoned up one Wednesday, three weeks ago now. 'Can I come across and see you?' This 72 year old lady, her two friends and her husband. The woman and her two friends went into the back office there. The husband said, 'Well... can I just have a walk round outside?' He came back to the door eventually. He said, 'Hey, look at this...' He bent his arm. I said, 'What's the matter with you?' He had walked about 6 yards into the big church. He got a shiver or a shake or something and he got instantly healed. So he came back and said, 'Look at this, I haven't been able to do this for 7 years.' Nobody else to blame but God. In an empty church!

The next week, there were two women who pulled up outside here. Joanna looked to see who it was. They got out of the car and bent down. She wondered what they were doing. They took their shoes off and did a dance out there. So Joanna went outside and said,

'What's happening?' One of these women just prophesied over her straight away without any introduction. And then the Spirit of God came on Joanna and so she had a prophetic word for them. And they all had a dance and a rejoice and they jumped back into their shoes, jumped in the car and off they went. Filled with the Holy Ghost. The original prophecy said that as some people step onto the premises they'll be healed!

FRUITS

Although he's a farmer, Jim has an insatiable curiosity and an intellect to match. In 1998, he set off on a round-the-world trip: "We went looking for why revival tarries." And then he lists some of the famous revivals from the past: Welsh, Hebridean, Wesleyan... But then he talks about some of the more recent ones: Toronto, Pensacola (Brownsville) and Lakeland.

Even Sunderland in the mid 1990s – Ken Gott who had been to Toronto and also Holy Trinity, Brompton began running meetings with Sunderland Christian Centre and things quickly grew until they were having meetings every night. People were collapsing in the aisles, shaking, laughing and God was doing powerful things in their lives. Billy Graham... Benny Hinn... J.John... They all came to Sunderland. But like everywhere else, after eighteen months or so, it was all dried up.

The first stop was Singapore. Between 1980 and 2010, the number of Christians in Singapore almost doubled. But nobody seemed to know anything about it. "Except we met a chap called C.K. Tang whose name is like Harrod's in Singapore – a multi millionaire. He got gloriously saved and bought the only cinema in Singapore to turn it into a church. But we didn't see anything of the revivals of the late 1990s and early 2000s.

Next stop: Cairns, Australia. The revival there lasted 18 months but there was no sound or sign of it. In Brisbane, there had been a revival in the 1920s, but again, nobody knew anything about it. In Sydney, there was a revival there in the 1940s and 50s. Where had it gone?

New Zealand was next after Australia, there had been a revival in Christchurch. Nobody knew anything about it there. Up to Auckland, nothing up there either; there was a revival at a place called Napier on the east coast of New Zealand.

The last stop was Fiji. When we were still in short trousers. There used to be a thing called the Juvenile Missionary Association in the Methodist Church [JMA is still going strong although is now known as Junior Mission for All; these days you can download the fund-raising chart and order the (plastic) badges online]. We were all given a collecting card for money to go to foreign missions. We even made the JMA promise: 'I promise to learn, pray and serve with the world-wide church of Jesus Christ.' Depending on how much we each raised, we got a little bronze [copper], silver [tin] or gold [brass] leaf to go on our medal.

It was all about raising money for the missionaries in other parts of the world. And so in 1946, we began to hear stories from the missionaries about a revival in Fiji so that's why we finished our trip in Fiji, in the middle of nowhere. I'm glad we did because that's where we found revival still going on.

Nearly sixty five percent of the country are practising Christians and most of those are Methodist. When the English took over Fiji in 1874, they brought thousands of Indians with them to work the sugar plantations. That accounts for most of the rest of the population - there are still a few temples dotted around.

We felt the difference before we even got off the plane. Instead of hurrying us off the plane as quickly as possible so they could go and have a cup of tea, people were welcoming us. No garlands or anything but a handshake. It's the only place I've been in the world where the atmosphere is different; completely different. They are the happiest people on earth.

The grandparents, some of the people who were alive during the original revival are still alive. The parents, the children and the grandchildren: everybody was so happy – whether the wizened old grandfathers or the young children.

That weekend happened to be a youth festival so the stadium was full of people, the adults were all throwing barbecues and there was a Christian band playing on the bandstand. Everywhere you went, there was Christian music playing out.

Why is revival still going on there and not elsewhere? We have too much. That's why. Every little group of people – nearly all villages, no big towns except there's about four towns that aren't very big. But people are still in their own villages by and large with a village chief that lives in a bigger house that's on stilts so you have to go up some steps to his place. Otherwise everybody lives in their wooden houses. There's no old fashioned mud houses or anything like that.

Interestingly, some sources list the principal religion here as Methodist, rather than Christian, which suggests that the Western Christian missionaries who arrived here in the 1830s were good Wesleyans. In each of the villages we visited we found a meeting place, a large room where, four times a week, the folk gathered for Bible study. No comfy chairs here, just little desks with an inkwell at the corner, like those I remember from my school days. The leader of the group had few resources at his fingertips, but he had enough: the Bible, a Concordance, and a copy of John Wesley's Journal and Sermons. And faith. Trusting the Father, praising the Lord, these uncomplicated Christians had learned how to enjoy their walk with the Lord, and revival had followed. And so it goes on.

We, on the other hand, have all the aids to building faith and encouraging prayer - videos, books, cassettes, seminars with high-profile preachers - yet we lack revival. To put it another way, even the poorest of us is materially wealthy compared to our Fijian brothers and sisters, yet spiritually they are the ones who are blessed with riches. Digging into the Bible, they have uncovered seams of gold, and they haven't been slow to mine them. I was intrigued to read in the tourist information that gold is among the commodities which Fiji exports. As we left that lovely place, our visit all too brief, I prayed that we might take some of their 'spiritual gold' with us as we headed back home.

And they want for nothing because they've got Jesus. The men sit at one side still and the women sit at the other side but they sing our old songs and all the old hymns and they're the happiest people on earth.

And Jim can't quite help himself but note how they farm:. "It's a dusty place and they're a bit backwards; they were still ploughing with oxen! But I've never seen people so happy and had such a warm welcome."

Jim is quick to tell me about all the times Hollybush has been on TV: Tyne Tees and national radio 16 times. The first time was in 1984, for 19 minutes for a show called Faith In Action – we were all in short sleeves in those days and we had hair! God said we'd be on television without payment.

The last one went national and international, It was September,

about 6 years ago and we have some friends over in America rang us up about midday our time said, "Eh, Jim, have you got the Daily Mail today?"

I said, "No, we don't get that."

He said, "Well you're on page three."

That went international and it was on all kinds of radio programmes and syndicated television. We didn't get a penny out of it of course. It was a lamb, born in September. And the greatest thing was it was the easiest testimony we've ever been able to give: just the same as Jesus, my best friend; born to die. The Lamb of God, died for our salvation. Everybody asked the same question and I gave them a straight answer!

The first time I sit down with Jim, he's quick to run through a list of people that need to be included in the book - people who were at Hollybush and went their own (sometimes very long) way to follow God's call on their lives.

The point of fruit is that you pull it off the tree and it goes somewhere else. So from that there's people all over the world. And people in England of course as well.

Kay's Farm: that's some more farmers up near Lancaster. They came here and got filled with the Holy Spirit. Then there's folks from Barnard Castle - there's still meetings going on there. And South Emsall and at Sunderland.

And then there's the work with the FGBM meetings and that connected with the Women's Aglow and the midweek meetings. We were going all over the place taking midweek meetings when people had midweek meetings.

There were two girls that came to a camp meeting all those years ago. They made a commitment to follow the Lord there and then. God told both of them that he wanted them in the Philippines in different places. Twenty five years on, they're still there with their families – they both married Filipino boys and are still there doing the job for Jesus.

One is Christine Hailes as she was but now Chrissy Perillo. Her video (from 2011) is available to watch on YouTube.[11] Chrissy went to Subic in the Philippines in 1983 as a missionary to give ten months of her life. She's been there ever since! To begin with, she spent much of her time ministering in the prisons, but her heart was moved when she saw so many children in there and she wanted to try to get the children out of prison and give them a hope and give them a future.

So in 1987 she started the Philippine Outreach Centre Children's Home which has now grown to 83 children. Out of the children's home, she and her team also started a school which they opened not only for their own children but also for children in the neighbourhood. The school now has 160 students.

Although there are 83 children in the home, some of the staff are former residents; they have grown up and are now working in the home or the school. "It's wonderful to see that over these many years that God is using our children, now as young people or young adults reaching out to others that are in a similar situation as they were."

The prison ministry is ongoing – they go into four prisons every week to share the love of Christ with the inmates who would normally have no visitors and no access to basics like toothpaste or soap to even wash their clothes. Chrissy counts it a privilege to be able to give some hope and to share the love of Christ the prisoners.

As with many ministries in the developing world, it's a constant battle between overwhelming need and finances that are never quite enough.

"We have thirty students and two teachers gathering together

---

11 https://www.youtube.com/watch?v=zAo

every Monday, Wednesday and Friday and they are interceding to save our school and we believe that God will do it. And we thank you for all your support in prayer because prayer is powerful and I believe it and we have seen it. And we believe that God is going to do great things. And even though our children's home is under threat of closure because the social services are requiring us to upgrade and we don't have the means to, but we believe in prayer and we believe that God will provide everything that we stand in need of. Even though it sounds bad, we still have a great vision. We are believing not only for God to save our school, but we are looking to expand so that we can accommodate 600 students because God is faithful and the need is great. And I believe that in these last days, God is going to use our young people, our children to reach the lost in these last days., And I believe that God is going to use P.O.C. [Philippine Outreach Centre] students to do it here in Subic."

What strikes me about these words is that they are so similar to words and sermons I've heard dozens of times from Jim and others who've preached at Hollybush. Believing, with perfect faith, that God can and will intervene when it seems like there is no hope.

Lesley Gomez set out as a Missionary to the Philippines on the same flight as Chrissy Perrillo. They ended up working in different areas and both wrote books about their incredible experiences. Have a Little Faith: Fixing Broken Childhood's In The Philippines Paperback by Lesley Gomez (Monarch Books) is worth a read and is still available to buy. [Chrissy's Book is called Living Under The Volcano (Kingsway)]

"Lesley's heart was broken at 22 by the hopelessness in the faces of little children struggling to survive extreme poverty in the Philippines. She had volunteered from England as a nurse for six months. Now, with her husband Peter (a Filipino pastor) she has devoted her life to serving the poor, venturing into dire situations to rescue child prostitutes, criminals, addicts and the homeless.

This book tells their stories, and through them the story of God's amazing ways as Lesley established Life And More Abundant Ministries, a charity for the relief of poverty, and Lama House, a residential home for abandoned, neglected or abused boys. The book is filled with graphic accounts: A violent gangster made tender; a suicidal addict snatched from the brink; a teenage daughter sold into prostitution; tragedy on a colossal scale in the great earthquake that hit Luzon. There are many horror stories, but again and again they are turned around for good."[12]

She wrote a few words especially to be included in this book:

It had all started at Keswick Convention in the beautiful Lake District of England. I was twelve years old, skinny and extremely shy, making my way to the front of a huge marquee packed with thousands of people, in response to the appeal at a missionary meeting. I signed a pledge on a printed piece of paper which I later pasted in my Bible as a reminder. It read:

"On July 17, 1973 at the Missionary Meeting at Keswick, I made my personal response to God's challenge to whole time service at home or abroad, signed: Lesley Keenan."

I had no idea where that strange courage came from that had me laying my life down, lock-stock-and-barrel. To do anything no matter how difficult, go anywhere for as long as it took was so uncharacteristic. It had to be God! Despite my young age I knew the commitment would cost me something and that it would be service abroad, but I had no idea where exactly. I had a vague notion that perhaps God would call me to be a missionary to the American Indians, perhaps because I had always wanted to own a horse!

Then two years later I met Reverend Clyde Shields and The Choir of Miracles at Hollybush Christian Camp in Yorkshire. They were travelling around the world to raise funds for their Bible College. I was enthralled by their music

---

12   Lesley Gomez, *Have A Little Faith*,
        Monarch, 2014

and the emotional stories Pastor Shields told of missionary work in the Philippines. The tears streamed down my face from the beginning of their concert to the end and when they moved on to another venue our family followed them all over the North of England.

At the end of August I celebrated my 22nd birthday, then two weeks later I was waving goodbye to my family at the airport. A girl my age accompanied me on the flight who I had been introduced to at Hollybush Christian Camp earlier that summer, her name was Chrissy Hailes. She was going to work as a missionary in Olongapo, near Manila. As she told me of her plans for prison ministry and her experience already in prison ministry in England, my own plans paled in comparison. At that time neither of us knew that we would be dedicating our entire lives to missionary work in the Philippine Islands. There was a lot that we didn't know.

Miracle Bible College was built on top of a hill, on the outskirts of the city of San Fernando. The steep road to the top was in poor shape but as the Jeep struggled upwards I was not concerned, I was distracted by the beautiful fuchsia coloured bougainvillea and huge red hibiscus flowers, the banana and mango trees. Climbing out of the uncomfortable Jeep, dirty and sweaty, I caught sight of the view overlooking the turquoise China Sea and the city beneath us with its jumble of rusty corrugated tin roofs and half finished buildings. It was all so fascinating, my dream come true!

Susanna walked with me back down the mountain to the "Mission House," where I would stay for the first few weeks with missionaries from Oklahoma. It was a fairly new bungalow with modern amenities, I wasn't sure if I felt disappointed or pleasantly surprised as I had half expected to be in a mud hut in the middle of the jungle! The tiredness and excitement caught up with me as Bert and Mary Brewster showed me to my room and left me to unpack my bags. Thankful, but suddenly exhausted, I flopped onto the bed and fell asleep.

When I woke up it was night-time, an orchestra of crickets were chirping outside my window, dogs were barking and cockerels crowing. For a moment I didn't know where I was! Then as jet-lag caught up with me I lay awake wondering what lay in store for me and thinking back to the events that led me to the Philippine Islands.

My eyes filled with tears again as I tossed and turned on my bed in the Mission House trying to rest. Since 1975 I had looked forward to visiting Pastor Shields and the choir in the Philippines, and now I was really here! But disappointment washed over me because Pastor Shields was not at Miracle, nor would he ever be again. He died of a heart attack four months before my arrival. The awful sense of loss was felt by everyone who knew him for years after his death, and I grieved for him as if he were part of my own family.

Jonathan Dunning is a name known by many locally. Jim tells me, "Put his name down – his dad was the station master at about three stops up in those days between Northallerton and Darlington. They have relatives up in Askrigg or Aysgarth. [In Yorkshire, that's how people are introduced – by where their people are from.] He was born again here, went away to uni and then to Bible college, was a year in Altrincham as a youth leader and then he came back here and was with us for about 20 years. Now he's the leader at Meadowhead Christian Fellowship in Sheffield. He's been there for 21 years and is on his third church plant."

Of course, Jim's story glosses over the best parts of the story. Jonathan and his two sisters both came to faith at Hollybush in 1968. They started a Christian Union in the old Northallerton Grammar School (now Northallerton College) along with half a dozen others who had been saved through Hollybush. The headmaster was a Methodist lay

preacher and because of the change that he saw in them all and through hearing their testimonies, he quit his job, went to Bible college and became a minister.

M.C.F., Jonathan's church has its roots in the Sheffield House Church movement and was one of five churches planted out in 1983. It still holds to its original vision: to see local people won for Christ. When Billy Graham visited Sheffield in 1985, the church organised buses to take local residents to Bramall Lane (Sheffield United's football ground) for the meetings and many people from the local estates became Christians.

Jonathan spent the best part of two decades at Hollybush, latterly working in the office which gave him a unique insight into the running of the farm, the church and the various ministries. He describes himself as Hollybush's number one fan and also its thorn-in-the-side. Like many in churches across the land, they see how things might be done differently and many is the time when Jonathan offers his advice to Jim about the future of Hollybush. Just like everyone I spoke to, he is certain that Hollybush has a future and wants to help in that where he can.

Continuing to flick through his address book, Jim continues, "And then there's Lowell Shepherd but he'll be more difficult to grab. He's out in Japan. He came here and was with us for about 4 years and then got married while he was still here. He was head-hunted by YFC and he was there for a time following Clive Calver. And then he went to YFC Far East so he's lived out in Japan ever since."

That's about as terrible an over-simplification of someone's life and ministry that you can get! YFC stands for Youth For Christ – not Young Farmers Club! Lowell Shepherd was born in Canada and his first job was as an advertising salesman with the Fraser Valley News Herald, in Langley, British Columbia. He worked in Mexico and then as a pastor on Saltspring Island (where quite by coincidence, some of the McKnight family emigrated to in the 1800s). A move to England saw Lowell working as the national director for British Youth For Christ and as executive trustee for Spring Harvest. It also saw him regularly at Hollybush Fellowship.

He has spent time living and working on four continents, most notably the warzones of Southeast Asia and the Balkans. He is also a published writer with seven books to his credit, including stories of heroism in Bosnia during the war and a travel book chronicling his journey though Japan by bicycle.

As Asia Director for HOPE International Development Agency, he resides in Nagoya, Japan. His involvement with HOPE began in 1978, when he went as a volunteer to the refugee camps in Southeast Asia, setting up feeding programs.

Lowell is a man shy of the limelight and rightly so – some of the work that they do in Japan and across Southeast Asia is sensitive and they turn down most opportunities to talk about their work in print, including this one.

Of course, that is all publicly available information, so doesn't break any confidence. However, here are some words from Lowell that aren't:

Hi Mark

Please pass on our love and greetings. We watched the Tour de France stages on television here in Japan with great interest, recalling many of those roads we travelled during the years we lived on the Farm.

[redacted for privacy]

But, that does not diminish our great love and lasting and endearing memories of Jim and Cynthia and all that they did for us.

Lowell Shepherd

What is clear is that everyone who speaks of Jim and Cynthia, whether prince or pauper, does so with affectionate memories both of the Wilkinson family and also of what God was doing during their time at Hollybush.

We just had the son-in-law here of Harry Westcott, a man who came to one of our camp meetings about 25 years ago. He caught the vision if that's the right word and saw what was happening here. When he went back home to Australia, his father died a year later and left him about a hundred acres of land right out in the outback. Today it has a large auditorium and lodges. They have camp meetings out there. He's now a man who is retiring and handing over to one of his daughters whose husband is a singer who was here with us.

The website of that ministry says, "Vision Ministries is led by Bishop Harry & Doreen Westcott who have been in Ministry for over 50 years both as pastors for 19 years firstly within the Methodist church and then the Uniting church. Joining Vision Ministries in 1981 they have led outreaches both nationally and across the world in an itinerant capacity. For six years they conducted those great Charismatic Conferences in all the capital cities of Australia. Now as well as birthing a local church called Vision Fellowship they also conduct National Camp Meetings in the 1100 seat auditorium called the Go Forth Faith Arena, Australia's Bush Cathedral on Mamre Farm.

It must be 20 odd years ago there were some people turned up in a coach one Friday night which often happened in those days. We didn't have a speaker but they turned up so they were the speakers. There was about 24 of them and they had different 40 gallon drums that had been cut at different heights and that was their band. Oh they were tremendous – before the days of recordings. Anyway the main thing was they all loved the Lord. They came from a state in India called Nagaland – right up in the top corner of India. At that time they were 92% Christian – a Christian country. Little people – about four feet high. No higher than five foot any of them. But the amazing thing that we observed was they seem to have eternal youth. There were three pastors with them and I think they were 75, 76, and 78. The youngest person was 15 but you couldn't tell which was which. Anyway that's a good story.

A couple of missionaries that we support are Philip and Vanlal Walters. Philip had been out in Thailand and worked out into Burma and India and of course went through Nagaland and met this lassie and they got married about four or five years ago.

Don Bell is the director of a Bible College in Naivasha, Kenya. Don is a part of Hollybush when he's around. Don has been through a lot of trauma: early on, the Bible school had only about 20 students and because of the tribal conflicts, he saw some of them smashed to pieces in front of him. They razed everything to the ground and disappeared into the bush. He had to start from scratch again and with the conflict those he knew had been killed, only two people turned up.

It has indeed been tough for Don, but he is holding firm to his vision: "Now there are many Bible Colleges, so what makes this one different? Well first I'm not too concerned about certificates and diplomas, but to disciple believers, especially pastors and leaders, and to train them in the ways of the Lord. This takes time and commitment. You can teach four hundred students at one time, but you cannot disciple each one. So we only take ten to fifteen students and work very closely with them."

"We do give certificates and diplomas but really they are simply an acknowledgement that the students have attended the course. At the end of the day it will be more about their hearts and faith in God that will reveal the fruit of their lives. This has been our blessing as we have seen such transformation in them. The Bible is both simple and profound. It is available for all people to understand if they are willing to seek God and believe."

So that's some of the different fruit of ministry around the world – people who have travelled and ministered God's Holy Spirit in diverse places. What of the fruit of God's Holy Spirit on the farm?

In Miracle Valley, Jim reflected on what God might have been doing in the 90s – it seemed as though they weren't seeing so many miracles, and those they did see needed a much greater persistence knocking on heaven's door. Many from the youth group had grown up and moved on and families were leaving the fellowship in their droves to go to New Life Baptist Church, down the road in Northallerton.

What did Jim conclude? "The answer, I believe, is that we were growing up. Seeing so many miracles, so often, was exciting and faith building, but, as we have matured, the Lord evidently wants us to walk by faith rather than by miracles. He also wants to see the fruit of the Spirit in our lives, and fruit has to be cultivated. As a farmer, I know that fruit, or a crop of any kind, comes at a price. Nothing worth having appears overnight, as if by magic. So when I read about the fruit that God wants to see in our lives - love, joy, peace, patience, kindness, goodness, faithfulness, gentleness, self-control - I know that, at some point, there will be a cost involved. We should not be afraid of that."

Of course, the passage from Galatians 5 is very familiar to many: "But the fruit of the Spirit is love, joy, peace, patinece, kindness, goodness, faithfulness, gentleness and self-control. Against such things there is no law."

We've heard about the fruit of Hollybush's ministry around the world to other people. What about the fruit of the Spirit in the lives of ordinary people who have faithfully come to the fellowship? I offer just two of the many stories I heard of the real fruit of the Spirit at work in the lives of the people.

Sid married at the young age of 78, just a couple of days before I spoke to him. As a baby, someone (perhaps his parents) tried to kill him – smashed his head in, stuffed his mouth full of soil and discarded him under a bush. Yet somehow he survived. It was a tough beginning and as a young man, he was a street-fighter and a thief. He knew his life wasn't in order. In confession, the best the local priest could offer was that if he had taken communion, then his soul was washed clean but Sid felt that just didn't ring true.

In his wonderful Geordie accent, Sid told me, "I'd done one or two things and I was planning some more bad things and I said, 'Me heart's wrong.' I was working at the Rowntree's fruit factory; we used to make Fruit Pastilles, Rolos, Yorkies... I heard of a meeting in the factory. When I was coming down the stairs, there was a notice with a red line and I wondered why the red line. I went up to it and I read 'Workers' Christian Fellowship.' That was the first time I ever read anything - I was brain damaged so I couldn't read. That was the first miracle.

I went downstairs and there was a corridor that was a quarter of a mile long. Men were walking up and down. I stopped one of them and says, 'Excuse me, do you know anything about this Workers' Christian fellowship?' He says, 'It's on tonight: Thursday night. Come along! He turned out to be the only Salvation Army man in the whole factory. Amazing, wasn't it?"

That night, I was walking along the road, going to the religious meeting. I prayed this prayer; I said, 'God, I know I'm going to hell. I don't want to go to hell. Will you forgive me my past? God forgive me my past and let us know I'm forgiven. Change us, cause I can't change myself. I've tried religion, I've tried everything there is to try.' And I said, 'I'm getting worse. Unless you change us, I can't change meself. And let us know I'm going to heaven and not hell. And if you do that, I'll follow you anywhere.'"

"The Holy Spirit of God hit me at the top of the head, went right through my body to my feet. As I came up, all the burden and guilt left me. And I floated into that factory. Such a joy! I was sitting in the back and there was a vicar preaching called Geoffrey Howard who used to be a

millionaire and gave it all up to be a vicar: seven pound a week at that time and his wife couldn't get used to not having servants! He was preaching and I couldn't sit still. I was boiling; bubbling! I jumped up and I said I've been saved coming to this factory. Some of them knew exactly what I meant. That's where it all started."

And then the story takes the direction that most stories at Hollybush do: "And then they hoyed [threw] us out of church." All too many stories that I heard at Hollybush told of being rejected by the church because of this new 'fanatical religion'. Jim's story at Sandhutton Methodist Chapel was only the first of many.

The story doesn't end there – just like Jim, with a new fervour for the Lord, Sid got involved in evangelism and won many souls to Christ – through his own ministry and also with his involvement with Reinhardt Bonnke.

But Sid's story finishes with a lesson to learn about the first piece of spiritual fruit: love. Sid spent almost forty years with his first wife and faithfully cared for her for fifteen years after two major strokes. It was not a marriage filled with love, even though this woman was the one to bring Sid to Hollybush in the first place.

When his first wife passed away, Sid made a pact with God that he thought was a foolproof way to never having marry again: "I said, 'The woman I marry will have loved me for a long time. And she will be totally 100% compatible with me in every area of my life.'"

Maud was one of the women that Sid knew at Hollybush but had never seen her as anything but a sister in Christ. He sold Maud a caravan but when he handed over the key, she sat him down and said, "I've got something to tell you. I've loved you for a long time."

Sid recalls, "That blew me to bits. The Holy Spirit came, took her love and hit my heart. This explosion took place and I saw her as she really was – beautiful. I felt deeply moved. So I was on one knee straight away, grabbed her by the hand I said will you marry me?"

"I thought my life was over when my wife died. I was with her for nearly forty years. I looked after her in a wheelchair for 15 years. I was determined not to marry again. The Holy Spirit taught me a lesson about love that day – that the love God has for us is bigger than the pain we've been holding onto."

Or Mary, who told me, "I just came to faith recently. I've been a staunch Catholic from being brought up. I went through a divorce which didn't go down very well with the Catholic church naturally. I remarried a lovely man, Thomas. He changed his religion for me to Catholic at the time. I lost him about 3 years ago to cancer. He were a wonderful person. He was a taxi driver in Thirsk when we moved here from Leeds. We've got four children, all grown up and grandchildren and great grandchildren."

"I went to my lowest point when I lost my husband. I were going to St. Mary's Church in Thirsk then because they were good to me over Tom's funeral and whatnot. Very helpful. I used to get the bus in the morning and go to Darlington and all over just to fill my day after Tom died. I had nobody in the house to talk to. I was taking it really, really badly. The bus drivers would say, 'Tom would be turning in his grave if he saw you with all that shopping.'"

"One day I was on my way to Darlington on the bus and then somebody who knew me tapped me on the shoulder and said, 'You're really down today, aren't you Mary?'" She said, 'Get off the bus with me here. You're not going to Darlington, you're coming with me. So I got off the bus at Hollybush and I thought, 'Here we go!'"

"I've never looked back. They've made me so welcome – not pushy. I didn't have to listen to this or listen to that. Not been 'brainwashed' as people say I've been. But I've had some terrible

things said to me over joining. My family have come in on it now thank goodness. Folks were ringing my family and saying, 'You better keep an eye on your mum you know, she's gone to this place.'

"My family came straight away and said, 'Mother, we're getting worried about you. You haven't got a boyfriend, have you?'"

I can't believe the change in me. I can't believe that instead of reading a love book and all these romance books I'm reading my Bible. And I haven't gone. It's just that I've changed and I think that in myself it's for the good. I've comfort and I'm not lonely when I go home.

And I've been... you're going to laugh when I tell you... One day I went to buy a windbreaker and I came back with a caravan. I talked to Jim about it, about how I'm feeling at home and about the atmosphere – it's as though I've got leprosy at home. I can be at the bus stop and they'll be saying, 'Is it happy-clappy day Mary?' And they say worse than that."

"It's been hard but I'm here. I've never been as looked after, never had as much comfort and prayers for me family are lovely. I've no regrets and whatever they've thrown at me at home, I'm here. Jesus has saved my life. I don't mind you knowing this: this time last year, I was in a refuge for ill treated women. I'd got down to drinking a bottle of vodka a day. Now I don't even have a shandy. And I sleep. No nightmares."

BLOSSOM: JOANNA AND GABRIELLA

Joanna's was a voice sadly absent in Miracle Valley, and by her own admission, she's been through the fire many times. Praise God, she's such an important part of life at Hollybush now. She alone has the unique perspective of being a 'child of the manse' so-to-speak. Everything that has gone on at Hollybush has always been normal but yet 'not normal' for her.

I found it exciting I suppose being in it. Of course, Irene came to live with us when I was still quite a young age. She's great, quite a character! She used to work in the laundrette and lived at Sandhutton with her mum. She used to do some work for mum and babysit for me back then. When we moved up here and her mother died, my parents took her in.

Back then, I remember a house brimming full of people. We had a huge table in the kitchen that was always full of people and food. When we had the meetings up in the big house, I remember people walking past my bedroom.

Some of the families who have been around since the old days like the Allisons tell stories about bringing their five kids along on a Friday night and putting them to sleep in mum and dad's big double bed while they were in the meeting.

I was more or less sent to bed; I think about Gabriella now, my nine year old. She comes on a Friday night but she messes about at the back – I was around but I also had a routine. That's where Irene stepped in quite a bit at the time with mum and dad being so busy.

What I do remember is the travelling all over the world: I went with mum and dad so I was always involved in the meetings there.

I had a London black taxi that used to pick me up for school. I went to the grammar school in Northallerton and I was picked up by a one handed cab driver. He used to collect me from the end of the road here. But I always felt a little bit different – all the others got the bus but it didn't come along this road.

At school, there were times when I was joked about, but I ended up going out with the head boy and he was a Christian as well who came here with his family. That worked wonders! I had three good friends who weren't Christians and I was the shy one, a little bit of an introvert. But I always had some good friends so it was bearable.

I started singing at quite an early age with a friend and we had quite an active youth group here in Hollybush. I ended up making three tapes! Who knows what a tape is these days?!?! We had a jazz band at one point from Hollybush going out to the pubs and singing gospel jazz music.

Jim starts the story of Joanna's wedding through the eyes of a proud father:

We had watched with pride as our lovely daughter had grown from a little girl into a young woman, and now she was to marry. There was, of course, much feverish planning by the female Wilkinsons, followed by endless letters, phone calls and personal visits in order to secure all that needs to be in place for the Big Day. As a mere male I was excused involvement in many of these duties, but I was nonetheless exercised in my thoughts as we moved ever nearer the day when I would be walking down the aisle with my only daughter to give her away. This sobering thought was my companion as I went about my work on the farm, a strange cocktail of joy and sadness giving rise to my own version of pre-wedding nerves.

Our girl had given us much joy over the years, and I was proud to be her dad, proud to have been the main male figure in her life. It's not easy for a man to let go of that, and I admit that I had one or two reservations about her choice, but those thoughts were eased by the knowledge that Joanna would be marrying a man she loved, and who loved her. So on balance - and accepting that it's quite natural for a father to wonder if any man is entirely good enough for his daughter - I laid my concerns to one side and simply continued to pray that Joanna's choice was the right one. At the end of the day, our main concern was that she should marry a man who would cherish his wife.

I proudly walked Joanna down the aisle before giving her away in a ceremony conducted by our local vicar, Rev. Ted Spiller. For all of us it was a very happy occasion, tinged with sadness of course as Cynthia and I handed on responsibility for our daughter to her groom. At the reception, we sat back and sighed. Joanna looked radiant, the blushing bride with a beaming smile. Her new husband looked like a prospector who'd just struck gold. Indeed, as far as her parents were concerned, he had.

"They look happy enough," I remarked to Cynthia as we watched them leave for the honeymoon. In fact they looked so happy that I wondered if I'd been wrong about my reservations. Probably dads just worry too much about their daughters, I reflected. Our little girl had long dreamed of being happily married, and from the look on her face that day it seemed her dreams had come true. Or, to put it in the Bible's terminology, it appeared Joanna was receiving the desires of her heart.

To hear Joanna tell the tale is harder to bear and the family are still at times raw with the emotion. As we edit the book, Jim tenderly protects his daughter by asking for a bit less detail in print.

Leaving home at the age of 21, Joanna headed for the bright city lights of Harrogate. A solicitor broke her heart and that was the catalyst to an abusive relationship with another man who she met in a nightclub that tragically ended in divorce. "I knew, I knew, I knew, I knew when I walked down the aisle. It sounds horrible, doesn't it? That night, I thought, 'You've done something that you can never get out of now – you're a Christian or at least you're meant to be a Christian, your father's a pastor...' That old chestnut!"

Jim took up the next part of the story in Miracle Valley:

Joanna turned up at the bungalow, far from the beaming bride we'd seen off on her honeymoon two years before. "I've been to see a lawyer," she announced. "I'm getting a divorce."

Trouble, we learned, had been brewing for quite a while. Our son-in-law apparently had a drink problem, which caused him to be violent. Joanna had put up with his behaviour for as long as was reasonably possible, and now she'd had enough.

Jim and Joanna both freely admit that the next part was a journey for them:

I couldn't blame her, of course, and it was essential that our daughter should remove herself from what had become an increasingly dangerous situation, but I was dreading having to tell the fellowship that our daughter's marriage was over. I had always believed, and still do, that marriage is for life, and I had stated my conviction publicly. Never had there been a marriage break-up in the Wilkinson family and I'd been proud of that. Now I had to swallow that pride and tell the folks that, sadly, my own child was divorcing.

The thought came to me that perhaps I was to blame; that I should have listened to the reservations I'd had about this union. But there was no mileage in that. What was needed now was for the family to rally round and support the lassie. She had already endured a lot of pain; we did not wish to see that added to.

Our hope, of course, was that the church family would also rally round, and in fairness many were sympathetic and supportive, allowing the love of Christ to flow through their hearts in a measure of caring and concern.

But not all felt that way. As the news got out, tongues began to wag, hands were thrown up in horror, and the brickbats started to pile up.

"You obviously haven't brought her up right."

"It's your fault; you shouldn't have let them get married."

"It's shameful. How will this look to the people we're trying to reach?"

At such times it's not easy to keep a smile on your face or in your heart. But this is life; sometimes it will be tough, and Jesus told us so. It's particularly tough because we have a formidable opposition in the world, the flesh, and other people. If that implies that some folks act like the devil, well, that's true. Going through a divorce – and it hurts the whole family, not just the couple concerned – is difficult enough. But the hurts are multiplied when criticism comes from other Christians. As the Lord's people we will receive opposition from the world, but we can put up with that because the Bible tells us to expect it, and even to rejoice in it, when we're vilified for Christ's sake. The spiritual armour doesn't always work against the barbed words of your brothers and sisters. The poisoned arrows sent out by our own seem to strike home with stinging effect, stabbing us in the back, for which the armour of God provides no protection (see Ephesians chapter 6).

I have never understood why Christians should sometimes be so hurtful to one another. As someone has said, the Lord's army is the only army which shoots its own soldiers. It's ironic but true that Christians occasionally do the devil's work for him, and probably we've all been on the receiving end.

The only redeeming factor in this, or in any attack, is the assurance from Scripture that all things work together for good to those who love God. In other words, what the devil intends for harm, the Lord uses for our good. That doesn't take away any of the pain, but it does give us hope, as well as the assurance that God knows and cares what is happening to us.

Joanna is circumspect with passage of time: "Fortunately at that point there were no children involved. There was a dog. He ended up giving the dog away!"

When we, the church, should have opened our arms and welcomed Joanna back to care for her and help her back to wholeness, we gossiped, back-bit and tried to get our heads around the 'theology' of it all. As though Jesus spent his time talking about what the Scriptures say and ignoring the needs of the broken and hurting.

Sadly, it wasn't the end of Joanna's trials.

I started to socialise big time in Harrogate with work colleagues and whoever I met. I was doing things that lots of people do in their teens; trying out all the things that we'd always been told never to do. It all threw me into a horrible place to be, and of course I felt I couldn't return back here because of what people were saying about me. Just like living in a goldfish bowl.

But I knew God and I cried out to Him when I needed him. If you're grounded initially, which I felt I was, in the word and I had given my heart and life over to Jesus – I remember it distinctly – if you have that foundation, actually you're still anchored to it, wherever you end up in life. There's always that pull. You know that you know in the back of your mind where you should be.

When I did eventually move back to South Kilvington, I thought I'd met Mr. Right. I thought he was the one but after getting my life on the straight and narrow again, he turned out to be a gambler and a liar from the beginning. He lied and stole from me and social services, the police and mental health professionals were all involved.

During the February when I was pregnant with Gabriella, I was in the back of a meeting here. I was wanting to get back to God. I was at a major crossroads. Of course, people were gossiping; I was pregnant out of wedlock, 'Another big mistake that Joanna's made. Oh, shock, horror!' But my heart was wanting to be back alongside my parents and God and being in the meeting.

During the meeting, I heard audibly, "Gabriella," which means 'woman of God.' I didn't know for sure until the last week when I had my final scan (I was forty – they pay a little bit more attention to you when you're older).

The midwife said, "I think you're going to have a girl." I thought "I'm having a girl! Yes!" because everybody had been saying, "Ooh you're having a boy!"

I've had lots of prophecy, "You're going to go to America, you're going to marry so and so, you're going to have a boy..."

'Even after the harshest of winters, still the blossom returns to the tree...'

"We might have gone through the Winter," speculates Jim. "The testimonies and the words that we are getting from people that don't know much about us as well as those who do all collate to say one of these moments there's going to be a real move again in a bigger way than we've ever seen."

What does the future hold for Hollybush? And does that future include the next generations of the Wilkinson family? It's a question that I've asked of every single person that I've met and interviewed in preparing this book. It's a question that isn't without controversy: several times in the past, people have come on board as a kind of 'succession planning.' Yet for one reason or another, things didn't go according to plan and those people moved on to other things. Although the circumstances were sometimes painful, Jim sent them away with his blessing.

Questions about the future are on Jim's mind now more than ever – more than anyone he's aware that he's not getting any younger. Not that he's showing it, of course! I joke with Joanna, "Somehow, Hollybush seems to have discovered the secret to eternal youth!" At least, I'm only half joking. The standard of what is old inside these gates is entirely different to the standard of what is old outside the gates. Jim is pushing 85 but he's in better shape than plenty of 70-year-olds that I know. It's a tough life, is farming. Even with modernisation, farmers have to work hard and by the time they're 65 most of them are riddled with arthritis and ready for their well-earned retirement.

By the sweat of your brow you will eat your food until you return to the ground, since from it you were taken; for dust you are and to dust you will return.[13]

Not only Jim, but men like Arthur, Edwin and Ernest who have ploughed this furrow for many years ought to be out to pasture by now.

We watched a DVD that we made in 2000 and I said that most of them look younger today than they did all those years ago. Someone said to me recently, 'It must be in the genes – you'll live a long life too.' Hey, I don't know about that.

One lady comes here for camp who's eighty five now. She looks fantastic – great hair, skin and everything. I said to

13   Genesis 3: 19

her, 'Come on, what's your secret?' I know what it is, but I wanted her to say it.

She said, 'Passion and purpose.'

They're always looking to see what's next. They've seen all the things God has done in the past and over the years and they've taken him at his word. God isn't finished here and so they all just forgot that they were growing older – they were just so wrapped up in what God was doing and is doing and is going to do next.

Jim and Cynthia are both becoming increasingly aware that perhaps they might not be around forever. Jim's had a couple of new hips and Cynthia is waiting for a new knee. And they are asking the question that every father and mother ask as they get older: what's going to happen to my child when I'm gone?

This last twenty years for each one of us for us that are getting a bit older... I got to sixty and then you find yourself at eighty four; twenty four years have passed. You get to sixty five, you get your pension and your bus pass. With us here, we've never noticed it. Whether we've been too busy or what, I don't know.

When anything happens to me or Cynthia, we want whatever Joanna wants. We don't want to force her into anything. She's come right back to the Lord. She's back working for the Lord now and she's got a vision for the place but we don't want her to be under any obligation if anything happens to us. And she knows that.

It's not an easy time at the moment because as you've noticed, we haven't got any young families. She's coming fifty and we don't want her or Gabriella killing off by any burden that might be put on her. She's half way through her life already. She has Gabriella who's nine going on eighteen! She needs to know exactly what God wants for her does Joanna.

It's not an easy job, running something like Hollybush so that's one of the things that we're trying to do is shield her from any pressures that she's going to have; you can't stop people back biting and things like that. We don't want to burden her with her if God hasn't called her to it.

To be clear, the question about the future of Hollybush is about succession. This is no morose speculation about what might happen after the big man goes to glory. Jim shows no signs of slowing down. In Joanna's words, "Dad's going to live 'til he's a hundred and ten, bar the rapture probably!"

There's two big questions that need answered for the future of Hollybush and they're so entwined, they're almost the same question. What happens to Hollybush Christian Fellowship? And what happens to the Wilkinson farms? After all, these are Yorkshire farmers. Like the Spences, the Breckons and every other farming family mentioned in this book and in Miracle Valley, the natural way of things is that the farm passes to the children. Joanna might not mind owning a farm (or two farms in this case – The Limes at Sandhutton and Hollybush), but I have a feeling she would be the first to admit she has no desire to jump up on the old Massey-Fergusson 135 tractor and cut silage!

But maybe the question isn't about what people are doing but rather what God is doing through his Spirit here at Hollybush. Maybe the question is what about God's anointing?

Margaret Brown has been around Hollybush since the very start; since her husband showed up on the farm trying to sell Jim farm supplies and fuel oil. Noticing a 'Praise The Lord' bumper sticker on Jim's car, he said, "So you're a churchgoer?" as an opening sales gambit. Well, that was like the famous, 'Is the pope a Catholic?'

Margaret is a wonderful, spiritual, praying and prophetic woman who almost managed to get herself onto the

Great British Bake Off. (Watch this space – she will almost certainly go for it again!) The story of how she and her husband Ian received God's spirit is well known – Ian felt like he was being torn apart, as if there was a battle going on for his very soul as he drove home from a meeting at Hollybush one night.

Interesting that one of the first things that Ian said to Jim was, "I'd like to introduce you to our range of oils." Why interesting? Because somehow by God's spirit, some of the oil that will be used to anoint the next monarch in this country has passed to the Brown family and anointing is a word that is on their lips constantly.

Margaret and her daughter Julie talk about the anointing that they received at Hollybush.

"In those, days, when we came to Hollybush and had those meeting in the upper bedroom, there was a sound of the worship itself. There would be songs but no OHP or instruments really. We would all just be singing but there would be such a sound. I think it was something that God invested in what he was birthing here. There was a very sensitive grasp of how to come into the worship of the Lord. And so they'd sing these songs that might just be four lines because people had to be able to remember what the words were. But that worship, you'd get on this journey and perhaps it was very attractive to the Holy Spirit. There's a connection; a powerful, powerful one and it may be the case worldwide but it's definitely true here. And so the connection between coming into this place where the worship that you're bringing is actually starting to activate things. The presence of God is drawn and it starts to shift the dynamic in the room."

"That was the environment that we knew and we knew it just by being in it as kids. I can remember talking to Uncle Jim about this probably about seven or eight years ago. I can remember saying to him, 'You know we'd be starting to sing and things would be starting to happen in the room... What is this?'"

"And he said 'Well it's the anointing lass!' He understood something but it had never been explained to me. In his mind it was a given that everybody else understood what he knew. I knew it by the feeling but I didn't understand it with my intellect. So when he said it that day, I thought, 'Oh my giddy aunt, of course it is!' So this feeling – it's not just a feeling it's the anointing. It's the actual presence of God coming into the place where you are."

"Some of the mega churches get rightly accused of being too glitzy. And part of that is that on a human level they're trying to reach for the 'sound' of real worship when actually you don't achieve the sound on a human level by making the guitar sound great and your lights look fantastic. It actually comes through a different avenue. In those early days, we had an organ. It's nice to have all the bells and whistles but you don't need all that. The churches would have a song leader ready to sing a few choruses. We've gone from that to, 'I'm the worship leader.' The worst scenario is because someone plays a guitar and sings well, they become the worship leader... That's just playing an instrument and singing songs. It doesn't matter how well you sing or strum a guitar. What matters is your heart and where your spirit is. If you've got a heart and a sensitivity to the spirit, that's what matters. If you have the anointing..."

The word 'anointing' is one that you'll hear regularly at Hollybush. Sometimes in the most unbelievable stories, like the 'golden glory' or 'golden anointing,' when a golden coin appeared on the forehead of a visiting speaker as a symbol of the Holy Spirit's anointing.

All that to bring us onto what the future might look like for Hollybush. Margaret Brown describes the past and future in terms of DNA. "Now, my family has a DNA. We can adopt you and I can call you my son but you don't have my DNA and you never can have. I'm talking about both spiritual DNA and also natural DNA. There's a spiritual DNA that we came to inherit coming along to Hollybush – we learned about the things of the Spirit and put them into practice in our lives. But we're only adopted into the family. We don't have the natural DNA of the Wilkinson family."

Margaret is fully aware of what she's saying here and it's an opinion that I've heard more than a few times as I've been around the Hollybush site. The people who hold the natural DNA of the Wilkinson family are Joanna and Gabriella. But Margaret knows that what she's suggesting isn't without its controversy.

"There are a faction who would say there's big sins and little sins and even bigger sins. Are any of us good enough? No. Should Joanna be taking a wider role in the leadership of Hollybush? I know that I know that I know that God chose her. Do you think now he says, 'Oh crumbs I've made a mistake? Look what she's doing!' No, he knew. He chose her."

I put Margaret's idea about the DNA to Joanna. She was quick to reply with just a hint of sarcasm in her voice, "But I'm a woman, and divorced...." Joanna has clearly faced no small amount of criticism before. She knows that although she has her supporters, it's not a universally held belief. She tells me a story of something that happened quite recently.

Someone had a pop at me in the last couple of months: 'Oh well, you're family – your dad is pushing you in. You're coming in through the back door.'

I was gob-smacked. I said, 'Do you really think I'm in this for me?' I was dumbfounded! In the natural, who would want this? It's not some great career move for me and my family. If I was doing this for me, I would take all my retail experience, go into Barker's and do a nice little nine to five job or better yet nine to three. I'd go home, pick Gabriella up from school and help her with her homework.

All I know is, since I've been here I've had a greater understanding of what goes on. It's a different experience from when I was a child. I've been in the back office, I've been with people, listening to them and I've watched how my dad works. I've felt that God's saying to me just hang in there and watch your dad - the traits, how he is with people, the decisions he makes, how he goes about it.

I know I go home but even then it doesn't always stop sometimes. Because my dad and I are together nearly 24/7, I feel that I've got a passion for the people. That's all I can describe. Now what happens from there, I don't know. Again, I'm a single parent. I don't have a husband. So people pair you up. Because getting married is the solution to everybody's problems!" [She says that last bit dripping with sarcasm].

But I know that I know that I know that for the moment I'm just standing. Not firm, but just standing; anchored. God will show me if he needs to show me whoever or whatever. At the moment I'm just gently going along but supporting my mum and dad.

I have absolutely no agenda at all. But if God has called you to something - if God has actually called me or whoever.... You know, there's been prophecies but if God has called you, you can try to fight it but it will only work for a while. But I know that I know that I know in my own heart that for my dad, I want to support them a hundred an ten percent in whatever decisions he has to make about the future.

There's a young couple I've got my eye on - nobody knows about at all - to think about coming. Again, no agendas, they're absolutely oblivious to my thoughts on their lives and it probably works better that way sometimes - don't tell people, just wait for God to tell them.

I do see a future, but I think we need to make some kind of arrangements. Not to be foolish – a future planned with God's help. I think dad's feeling that too.

As of this moment, there have been no decisions made as to the future leadership of Hollybush. It may be Joanna, it may be someone else or even a group of people. But there's one thing that is certain: for anybody who has spent the shortest time in the office with Joanna, it's clear that she is indeed back with the Lord and has a heart to serve him.

Margaret Brown was the one to connect anointing with heart: "It doesn't matter how well you sing or strum a guitar. What matters is your heart and where your spirit is." It almost sounds like a sermon from George Breckon or from Jim himself. Perhaps we might put it another way: it doesn't matter what your past is. Where you've been, who you were with, how it all went down. What's in the past should stay there and we have an incredible God in the here and now who has shown time and again that he forgives and intervenes with supernatural power in people's lives.

Can God heal a broken body? There a literally hundreds of stories from Hollybush over the years that would most emphatically say, "Yes, a thousand times, yes!" From Jim Wilkinson's dive over his handlebars as a child to Bernard whose foot was healed just a couple of months ago, the folks at Hollybush will testify that God's Holy Spirit is real, He's at work in this world and is in the business of healing. And hopeless cases are what God specialises in.

There's a phrase that comes back again and again in Scripture: 'How much more...?' If God can heal a broken body, then how much more can heal heal a broken heart, a broken spirit and a broken past. Hebrews 9:13-14 says,

Under the old system, the blood of goats and bulls and the ashes of a heifer could cleanse people's bodies from ceremonial impurity. Just think how much more the blood of Christ will

purify our consciences from sinful deeds so that we can worship the living God. For by the power of the Eternal Spirit, Christ offered himself to God as a perfect sacrifice for our sins.

So if God's will and his anointing do indeed rest on Joanna, then we jolly well better get behind that. Because the testimony of Hollybush as a people is that the miracle-working God through His Holy Spirit can heal all things. And if God's anointing rests on someone else, then we'll tell Joanna how wonderful she is and then get behind that person. Anyway, I'm not quite sure how we would go about finding a new senior pastor. Perhaps an advertisement like this one?

The Perfect Pastor

The perfect pastor preaches exactly 30 minutes. He condemns sin roundly but never hurts anyone's feelings. He works from 8am until midnight and is also the church janitor.

The perfect pastor makes £40 a week, wears good clothes, drives a good car, buys good books, and donates £50 a week to the church. He is 29 years old and has 40 years experience. Above all, he is handsome.

The perfect pastor has a burning desire to work with teenagers, and he spends most of his time with the senior citizens. He smiles all the time with a straight face because he has a sense of humour that keeps him seriously dedicated to his church. He makes 15 home visits a day and is always in his office to be handy when needed.

The perfect pastor always has time for church council and all of its committees. He never misses the meeting of any church organization and is always busy evangelizing the unchurched.

The perfect pastor is always in the next church over!

If your pastor does not measure up, simply delete the church at the top, add your own church to the bottom and send this notice to six other churches that are tired of their pastor, too. Then bundle up your pastor and send him to the church at the top of the list.

If everyone cooperates, in one week you will receive 1,296 new pastors.
One of them should be perfect![14]

It's tongue-in-cheek, of course. But reading that short poem, it's obvious that the 'perfect pastor' would be so bland that he'd be worse than useless. Are we going to find a perfect replacement for Jim when he retires? Here's the person specifications:

---

14   Author unknown, from the Rochester Courier Journal, September 1981

Hollybush Christian Fellowship
Vacancy: Senior Pastor

PERSON SPECIFICATION

Essential Qualities:	Desirable Qualities:
Anointed Beyond anything else, someone who the current leadership feels has been anointed by God's Holy Spirit to fulfil this role	**Agricultural** Experience of mechanised arable and livestock farming in a rural Yorkshire context. Because as we all know, if it's outside Yorkshire, it's not worth visiting!
Spirit-Filled Someone with a lifetime of experience in seeing the Holy Spirit at work. Someone for whom the gifts of the Spirit are 'normal' - a part of their everyday faith experience.	**Clean Driving License (With Tractor Entitlement)** Experience in driving heavy plant and farming equipment. At interview, there will be a written examination on the proper use of a disc plough, a rotary tiller, a potato harvester and a threshing machine followed by a short practical tractor handling test.
Communicator/ Preacher/Teacher As we know, preaching is the **most** important of all the gifts that God has to offer. It's why we revere preachers so much and forget those who are constantly on their knees in prayer. Probably a good preacher is what we want more than anything else. Not someone who goes on for too long, mind. About half an hour is right, so that we can get home in time to watch Strictly Come Dancing.	**Good-Humour** The successful candidate will probably have deeply ingrained laughter lines at the corner of their eyes. And they will be all the more beautiful/handsome because of them. Stop using that Oil of Olay and forget the Botox – laughter is good. Especially when it's Holy Spirit inspired laughter.

Leader Of course, this is self-explanatory. Although our people won't always like how they're being led so will probably gossip behind your back.	**Long-Suffering** God, grant our future pastor the serenity to accept the things they cannot change, The courage to change the things they can, And the wisdom to know there's much more in the first category than the second.
Pastor Someone who's never too busy to spend time with all-comers. Someone who always seems to have time to leave their desk and pray with anyone who needs it. Someone who knows when it's the right moment to comfort and and also to challenge.	**Time Management** Duties will include preaching and teaching several times a week. In addition we are currently without a youth pastor, so the pastor will also be *temporarily* responsible for all youth activities. The pastor will also responsible for all hospital, housebound, sick and pastoral visitation of members, former members, close friends of either as well as any family of the above who are 4th cousin twice removed or better. Also management of two farms and a haulage business (see below).
Administrator An encyclopaedic knowledge of the fellowship and two farms will help. You will be expected to know everything at a moment's notice and to never forget a name, date or appointment. And for your desk to be tidy, all the post to be answered and for each email to have a response within fifteen minutes.	**Yorkshireman** Let's face it, no one really understands Yorkshire folks... like Yorkshire folks. There's simply no possibility that someone could come from elsewhere and lead us. They don't know our ways. They don't know how we do things round here.

Experienced

It's important that our pastor has some 'life experience' - perhaps as a primary school teacher or accountant or something like that. Somebody who knows what it is like to live in the real world. It's most important to us that our new leader has faced the problems that everyday people face.

Squeaky Clean

While we are believing for a new senior pastor with 'life experience,' it's also important that there is no hint of moral failure in his/her past. This includes (but is not limited to): illegal drugs, sexual experimentation, financial irregularities, idolatry, drunkenness. blasphemy, fornication, witchcraft, murder... Oh and family problems. They need to have a perfect family because as we know, anyone who has problems in their family is clearly **very** sinful.

Inspirational

I mean, who doesn't want an inspirational pastor, right? Not so inspirational that we're all going to have to go off to the jungles of Borneo or anything – just someone who will tickle my ears enough that I'll think I'm going along well with the Lord and don't need to change much.

Personal Attributes

White, male, 50+, heterosexual, non-drinker, Yorkshireman, wears a tie. We are less concerned about more important attributes of character like depth of faith, honesty and integrity.

Missional

Someone with a heart for the lost.. blah, blah, blah... All that stuff. Of course they will have to go off and do it all themselves. We're all much to busy keeping the church going to get involved with 'outsiders.'

Likeable

Our final choice will most likely be emotionally biased or based on arbitrary circumstances like whether you wear a shirt and tie or not. We have fairly sketchy HR procedures so it's important that when we meet you, you're as likeable and inoffensive as possible.

Salary: You will be expected to manage two farms and a haulage business. There will be no direct remuneration for the role as senior pastor.

Working Hours: Negotiable. You will have to fit these in around work on the farm. Long hours and working under pressure (especially in emergency situations) will be expected.

Holidays: As with all farm work, it will be difficult for you to take holidays. In spite of what you are entitled to, there will be never ending demands on your time both on the farm and in ministry.

The successful candidate will also be expected to meet the criteria for leadership with regards to standards of conduct in both personal and public life and personal commitment to grow in spiritual knowledge and maturity. Members of the fellowship will monitor this closely and have been known to self-righteously and publicly call attention to real or perceived failures. You will most likely be the last to hear about this, after the gossip has done the maximum damage.

In accordance with Section 9 of the Employment (Sex Discrimination) Act 2000, this post <u>does not</u> qualify for an exception. Legally, there is no Genuine Occupational Qualification and therefore we have no grounds for demanding that the post-holder should be a man. Persons of any gender are welcome to apply.

Of course, that person specification is flippant and a little irreverent but in every piece of sarcasm, there's a grain of truth. Change is big and change is frightening, especially when it challenges what we thought was true. We want things better, but we don't want to have to change to get there. The truth is, we're not going to find a perfect replacement for Jim when he retires. In fact, we're not even going to find an imperfect replacement for Jim when he retires. Hollybush might look new and different in the future. Maybe even scary.

There are two questions about the future of Hollybush: one of general direction and another of leadership. I hope the person specification above makes you a little bit angry, because they're all attitudes that I've come across at Hollybush in different guises.

Some of the people I spoke to talked about two factions in Hollybush. The first group are the people who talk a good talk but want Hollybush to be their church. Somewhere nice and comfortable where they can go on a Sunday morning, sing through the old songs and go home to their roast dinner. (With Yorkshire puddings, obviously!) Miracle Valley spoke of the original prophecy, retained in full in the introduction to this book: "I will bring people here from the north, south, east and west to minister to you and to be ministered to. You will be a lighthouse set on a hill, and people shall come and be blessed of me, and return to their respective places of abode and worship to share what they have received." Hollybush was never meant to be a church – people would come in and then go out again. It's not from Scripture and its authorship is unknown, but there is a famous story know as the parable of the lighthouse (or the life-saving station). Perhaps it's particularly apt in considering the future of Hollybush.

> *On a dangerous sea coast where shipwrecks often occur there was a once a crude little life-saving station. The building was just a hut, and there was only one boat, but the few devoted members kept a constant watch over the sea, and with no thought for themselves, they went out day or night tirelessly searching for the lost.*
>
> *Many lives were saved by this wonderful little station, so that it became famous. Some of those who were saved, and various others in the surrounding areas, wanted to become associated with the station and give of their time and money and effort for the support of its work. New boats were bought and new crews were trained. The little life-saving station grew.*
>
> *Some of the new members of the life-saving station were unhappy that the building was so crude and so poorly equipped. They felt that a more comfortable place should be*

provided as the first refuge of those saved from the sea.

So they replaced the emergency cots with beds and put better furniture in an enlarged building. Now the life-saving station became a popular gathering place for its members, and they re-decorated it beautifully and furnished it as a sort of club.

Less of the members were now interested in going to sea on life-saving missions, so they hired life boat crews to do this work.

The mission of life-saving was still given lip-service but most were too busy or lacked the necessary commitment to take part in the life-saving activities personally.

About this time a large ship was wrecked off the coast, and the hired crews brought in boat loads of cold, wet, and half-drowned people.

They were dirty and sick, and some of them had black skin, and some spoke a strange language, and the beautiful new club was considerably messed up. So the property committee immediately had a shower house built outside the club where victims of shipwreck could be cleaned up before coming inside.

At the next meeting, there was a split in the club membership. Most of the members wanted to stop the club's life-saving activities as being unpleasant and a hindrance to the normal life pattern of the club.

But some members insisted that life-saving was their primary purpose and pointed out that they were still called a life-saving station. But they were finally voted down and told that if they wanted to save the life of all the various kinds of people who were shipwrecked in those waters, they could begin their own life-saving station down the coast. They did.

> *As the years went by, the new station experienced the same changes that had occurred in the old. They evolved into a club and yet another life-saving station was founded.*
>
> *If you visit the sea coast today you will find a number of exclusive clubs along that shore. Shipwrecks are still frequent in those waters, only now most of the people drown.*[15]

The second group or faction are the people who are still pressing in, still waiting for what God is doing. They're still clinging on to His promises and still holding Him at His word that His Holy Spirit will continue to move in power. You see, Hollybush was always meant to be a life-saving station or a lighthouse. That's what God told them in the beginning and on the basis that He hasn't offered any further information, Jim is working on the assumption that it all still applies. Hollybush was never going to be a mega church or meant to take people out of the world into a little Christian bubble.

They're the people who know that life-saving is their primary purpose. While a nice, big, warm church building is a wonderful blessing, what they care about is taking the name of Jesus to the world and reminding them that we serve a powerful God.

For Hollybush to grow, move forward and continue to become what God wants it to be, every one of us needs to humbly get on our knees and listen to what the Lord is saying. Not what the Lord said fifty years ago but what He's saying right now. And we need to take what we hear and offer it to the people that God has anointed to be our leaders. I can tell you beyond a shadow of a doubt that each one of them is on their knees every day doing the same thing: listening to what God has to say to them as individuals and to us as a people and a community.

---

15 Author unknown, adapted by Steve Rudd http://www.Bible.ca/evangelism/e-parable-life-saving.htm

And guess what? We won't all hear the same thing. Some of us will be misled by our own prejudices and by the things that have been ingrained in us since we were children, whether right or wrong. Some of us will hear things that disagree with what eventually happens. That's not to be feared: we test all prophecy as we're told to in Scripture.

There is one universally held belief at Hollybush and that is that Jim's godly leadership under the Holy Spirit for half a century in this little corner of Yorkshire has led to wonderful and powerful things.

There will come a day, maybe before too long, when the leadership at Hollybush has to make some decisions about the way forward and we might not like them. I might not like them. But I'll tell you what: each and every one of us will have a choice. We can choose to believe that Jim was a great leader up until his very last decision when he fell from grace. Or we can remember that this incredible man of God has been listening to the still small voice for much longer than we have and get behind whatever that decision is one hundred and ten percent.

And then we have a choice in how to respond: by getting behind what God wants to do with Hollybush in the future, by turning our backs and walking away; voting with our feet, or worst of all, staying as one of the detractors; bringing destruction and disunity instead of life and peace. Perhaps some pruning is just what's needed. Lord let me not be one of the branches that is cut off and cast into the fire. But don't let me be that guy: the one who stays and gossips, bringing the leaders down and finding fault. Let me walk away before I become that guy!

In all my conversations, there is nobody who has suggested that Hollybush doesn't have a future. Perhaps before any decisions are made, God's asking each one of us, "Are you in or out?"

I can see in Jim's eyes, in the way he talks and the way he preaches that this prophecy is foremost in his mind. Hollybush is just a little place on the back road between Northallerton and Thirsk but its impact on worldwide Pentecostal Christianity has been profound. By farming standards, it's about average in size. Yet somehow the stories of what God has done here keep coming: stories like the British missionary who found one of the 32,000 copies of Miracle Valley in a remote Nepalese church, two days walk from the nearest road.

And in almost our very last conversation before the book goes to print, Jim steers the discussion away from what God is doing at Hollybush and towards what God is doing in the lives of individual believers. In my life; what is the Holy Spirit doing in my life right now?

When the first book came out, Jim prayed that just one person would come to know the Lord through reading the book. On the morning it hit the shelves, Jim had a phone call from a woman who was the cleaner in a Christian bookshop. She had found the book the previous evening, read it and given her life to the Lord on the spot.

So our prayer isn't for just one person to come to know the Lord from this book. Our prayer is that hundreds would come to know Him. Thousands. Millions even! We pray that you have been blessed by reading *this* book. We pray that God is at work in your life. We continue to expect God to break through with his miracle-working power. And most of all, in Jim's own words we want to remind you, "Jesus Christ, the same yesterday, today and forever. He's alive. Get to know him. Make sure you know the Lord. Make sure that he's your best friend and keep him that way, because there's nobody else will touch him."

And we pray that having read our stories, you're able to pass them on with your own story – buy another copy of the book and send it to that one person who needs to hear these stories. Tell them your story too. And hopefully they will soon enough have a testimony of their own.

With grace and peace,

Jim Wilkinson & Mark McKnight

ACKNOWLEDGEMENTS

Hebrews 12:   1-2 (NIV)

Therefore, since we are surrounded by such a great cloud of witnesses, let us throw off everything that hinders and the sin that so easily entangles. And let us run with perseverance the race marked out for us, fixing our eyes on Jesus, the pioneer and perfecter of faith.

Some of the great cloud of witnesses that have fertilized my spirit:

Gladys Aylward, Helen Roseveare, Duncan Campbell, George Verwer, Tom Butler, C.R. Ransome, Arthur Skevington-Wood, Bill Davies, Jean Darnell, David Carr, David Shearman, Art Sheppard, Russell and Betty-Lou Mills, Melvin Banks, Kit Calvert, Peter Whiteside, Mervyn France, David Brown, Lewis Staley, with many other warriors and their families.

> For   when   the   One   Great   Scorer   comes
> _____To   mark   against   your   name,
> ___He   writes - not   that   you   won   or   lost -
> _But HOW you played the Game.
>
> From the poem, "Alumnus Football"
> _by Grantland Rice

Can we help you?

If through reading our story you have been blessed and feel that we could be of further help, please contact us.

We will be only too pleased to pray for you or to offer you counsel in the Lord.

Yours in the love of Jesus.

Jim & Cynthia Wilkinson

Hollybush Farm

Newsham, Thirsk

North Yorkshire

YO7 4DH

Tel: 01845 587386

Email: hbcfoffice@gmail.com

Web: http://www.hollybushchristianfellowship.co.uk/